HOW THE COMMUNISTS USE RELIGION

HOW THE COMMUNISTS USE RELIGION

by *Edgar C. Bundy*

Author of "Collectivism in the Churches"

THE DEVIN-ADAIR COMPANY

NEW YORK   1966

DEDICATION

To Bea and Bart Richards, Anne and Dillon Winship, Nancy and Rogers Follansbee, J. Howard Pew, Walter Knott, Dr. and Mrs. Anderson Arbury whose constant encouragement inspired the author.

CONTENTS

22934

CONTENTS

INTRODUCTION

Ever since the publication of my book *Collectivism In The Churches* in 1958 a great debate has raged throughout the United States from pulpit and pew, in secular and sacred newspapers and magazines, over radio and television, on the floor of the United States Congress, and around the dinner table on the subject of whether or not the Communists have actually been using churchmen to further the objectives of the Soviet Union. To the headquarters of the Church League of America in Wheaton, Illinois have come untold thousands of news clippings which have contained "Letters to the Editor", syndicated columns consisting of affirmations and denials, bristling sermons from indignant clerics, and far out diatribes against "extremists", "smear artists", "divisive forces", "discredited" this-and-thats, "splinter groups", "patriots-for-pay", "literalists", "fundamentalists", and a host of other labels, the use of which was intended to distract the listeners' attention from the issues and the facts. More heat has been generated in this eight year period than light.

In a court of law, or under oath before a United States Congressional Committee, a witness is held responsible for everything he says, legally. There is such a thing called perjury, which means telling a falsehood under oath, resulting in a prison sentence. Also, in such proceedings, exhibits are entered into the record in the form of documents and original items. Gossip is not admissible. Ignorance of facts is soon exposed. That is why some, who wrap themselves in ecclesiastical robes, may say one thing from the pulpit or seminary chair, but who will not repeat it in legal proceedings where they would be held accountable.

What is left of the Free World is engaged in a titanic struggle with an awesome Force which has vowed to destroy and to destroy until it conquers the entire globe. It is a satanic force, built on atheistic materialism; *BUT*, seldom does it show its true face or intent to those whom it intends to conquer. It comes dressed even "as an angel of light", to use the words of Holy Scripture. It uses such words as "peace", "unity", "brotherhood", "neighborliness", "togetherness", "social progress", and even "love".

Behind the front or façade, is the poison of the asp. This movement has a vocabulary of its own which gives to dictionary and Biblical words and phrases a meaning opposite from the true definition.

This force doesn't stand on a soap box in Bughouse—or Union Square—screaming "Comes the Revolution", dressed in disheveled clothing, or wearing long whiskers and frizzy hair, a six-shooter in one hand and a bomb in the other. More times than not its spokesmen have been near geniuses, though evil ones; university graduates with strings of academic degrees; brilliant philosophers; artists, sculptors, writers, musicians, political demagogues, scientists, psychologists, linguists, and, surprising to some, religious leaders in high places. History is replete with these types. The Force has never been led by, nor has it appealed to, the common masses of people who simply want to earn and to eat their daily bread, and raise their families.

It has been an elite corps from the beginning: the planners and controllers who have an insatiable lust for wanting to pour the masses into their mold, and then to manipulate them as a device for gaining worldly power and position.

Since the publication of COLLECTIVISM IN THE CHURCHES in 1958, this Force has marched steadily onward. It has not retreated one inch. Despite all the blood of Western lives shed in Korea, the 38th Parallel remains the dividing line between a free and a controlled Korea. Despite all the billions of foreign aid money sent to Europe by the United States the divisive line runs through Germany with a free Republic on one side and a communist satellite on the other side; and, something new has been added, a wall to divide Berlin. Cuba is in the hands of the Communists. Its leader snorts fire and brimstone at the United States in day-long harangues, ninety miles off the American coast. The island has become a training ground for the exporting of Marxist revolutionaries to all of Latin America. Protestant missionaries who praised Fidel Castro when he took over Cuba, are now in Castro's prisons.

Thousands more Russian churches have been closed in this eight-year span. Native leaders in Africa, trained in U. S.-sponsored mission schools, have become the Communist leaders in that continent.

The most shocking development of all has been that Western Liberal clergymen have welcomed into their fellowship, through the World Council of Churches, Communists in religious garb; have defended them, and have elected them to church offices, even after the Red puppets had denounced the Western World in the most inconceivable lying terminology that an unregenerate soul could phrase, and had vociferously defended Soviet actions in Hungary, Korea, East Germany, Cuba and Africa.

Although it has been a wearisome job reading through the thousands of papers, books, documents, proceedings and diatribes of the Red clergy for the past eight years, it is hoped that this labor will not have been in vain because of the documented facts which are available in the pages that follow to all those who will take the time to absorb them.

A nation which is kept enlightened and informed will never succumb to the godless Force. Totalitarianism feeds on keeping people in the dark. Liberty and freedom thrive on bringing all things to the light!

The Soviet Empire and the Western World were rocked and shocked by the revelation in 1963 that Colonel Oleg Penkovskiy, Russian war hero, Senior Officer in Soviet Military Intelligence, graduate of the Soviet Staff College and the missile academy, had been voluntarily spying for the United States and Great Britain on a scale unprecedented in the history of modern espionage. Colonel Penkovskiy single handedly sabotaged Khrushchev's threatened Berlin showdown in 1961, and he supplied President Kennedy with the information of Soviet-Cuban missiles which caused the United States to defeat successfully the Soviet-Cuban threat in October 1962.

Penkovskiy's work for the Western World has been evaluated as "the greatest intelligence coup of modern times" by international intelligence experts.

Perhaps of even greater value than actual spying activities of Colonel Penkovskiy are the papers which the Colonel wrote in secret and which recently were smuggled to the West and were put in print by Doubleday and Company in 1965 in the form of a documentary of some 411 pages entitled *The Penkovskiy Papers.*

Colonel Penkovskiy brings irrefutable evidence to light concerning the role being played by the Russian Orthodox Church and the other major religious groups within the Soviet Union as government agencies for the dissemination of communist propaganda. Here are Colonel Penkovskiy's own words:

"Here is a list of some of the Soviet ministries in various committees through which we conduct intelligence and where we (i.e., the GRU and the KGB) have our representatives; some of these state institutions are completely staffed with KGB or GRU personnel:

Council for the Affairs of Religious Sects, under the the Council of Ministries, USSR.
Council for the Affairs of the Russian Orthodox Church."

Here is the most significant statement of all from Colonel Penkovskiy's papers in regard to Patriarch Aleksiy's (Ruler of the Russian Orthodox Church) role in working with the Soviet Secret Police and the Kremlin:

"I remember that Varentsov once told me a very interesting story about two officers, a major and a lieutenant colonel, who were discharged from the Army and had no jobs. Both were engineers and they had been fine officers in the Soviet Army. They went to see Patriarch Aleksiy and told him they wanted to become priests. Patriarch Aleksiy, who has a direct line to the Kremlin, called Zhukov and told him: "Comrade Marshal, I have here with me two officers who want to become priests." Zhukov answered: "Send them to me, and thank you for letting me know about this." This happened a year before Zhukov's trip to Yugoslavia.

Zhukov saw the two officers personally. They told him the whole story, and Zhukov reinstated them in the Army. After that, Zhukov wrote a detailed report to the Central Committee and asked that the two officers not be arrested and that no drastic action be taken against them. For there might be other cases like this one and after all they were good officers. The officers stated that in a legal sense they had not done anything wrong because they knew that according to the Soviet law and the Constitution all clergymen in the Soviet Union are communists and work either under the Central Committee CPSU or in the KGB. Why, then, could they not be priests? Besides, there is a special committee under the Council of Ministers of the USSR which is responsible for all church affairs—a state institution. Everybody in Moscow was talking about this case."

Here is, without a doubt, the most important supporting evidence on the communist clergy of the Soviet Union which has yet been revealed. How will the Western liberal clergymen, who believe they can do business with the Russian clergy, answer this?

E. C. B.

Wheaton, Illinois

HOW THE COMMUNISTS USE RELIGION

Chapter I

THE RELIGIOUS FACE
OF COMMUNISM

"Woe unto them that call evil good, and good evil; that put darkness for light, and light for darkness; that put bitter for sweet, and sweet for bitter! Woe unto them that are wise in their own eyes, and prudent in their own sight!"—Isaiah 5:20, 21

On October 25, 1962 the official news agency of the Soviet Union, TASS, released a dispatch in English to all of Europe at 8:57 p.m. This was not an ordinary government-originated propaganda communique. It was an amazingly vicious blast against the United States of America coming straight from the recognized religious leaders of the USSR.

The date of the release was most significant. It was timed to counter the courageous move of President John F. Kennedy who had ordered Fidel Castro to remove his "Made in the USSR" guided missiles, pointed at the heartland of

the United States, out of Cuba or else have them forcibly
removed by means of the combined air, ground and sea
powers of the American armed forces.

The text read as follows:

Moscow—The heads of the churches and religious associations of the Soviet Union have issued an appeal to
all heads of all Christian churches and all Christians of
the world, urging them to do everything in their power
to prevent the disaster of war. The appeal notes that
mankind is now threatened by the outbreak of a world
war as a result of the actions taken by the U. S. administration against the Republic of Cuba which are extremely dangerous to the cause of peace.

We cannot but declare to the whole world that the reck-
less steps of the U. S. Government are a crying violation
of Christian teaching and a great sin before God, the appeal says. The appeal has been signed by Aleksiy, Patriarch of Moscow and all Russia; Vasgen I, Supreme Patriarch and Catholicos of all Armenians, Yakov Zhidkov,
chairman of the All Union Council of Evangelical Christian Baptists and others.

In addition to this vicious blast by the "big three"
religious leaders of the USSR against the American Government, Patriarch Aleksiy of Moscow and All Russia sent a
personal cablegram to U Thant, Secretary General of the
United Nations, at 8:15 on the morning of October 26,
1962 in which he loosed another unfounded attack on the
United States as follows:

On behalf of the Russian Orthodox Church I ask you
to do everything possible for the United Nations to ful-
fill its sacred duty in the preservation of world peace,
which at present is threatened by the actions of the U. S.
Government, directed against the sovereignty of the Republic of Cuba, which are dangerous to the cause of
peace. I express the hope for a successful result of the
peaceful efforts of the United Nations.

Both of these propaganda attacks against the American republic by USSR religious heads are in need of analysis at this point.

The prestige of all the religious groups of the Soviet Union is used to lend weight to the attacks upon the United States.

All the Christians of the world are appealed to.

Mankind (all human beings of the world) is threatened, we are told, *not* by the Soviet manufactured missiles installed on their launching pads in Red-held Cuba and poised for delivery to America's great cities, but rather by the American Government's order to Castro to remove them!

No mention is made by these religious wolves in sheep's clothing of the missiles' threat to countless millions in the United States. For some reason or other, this is conveniently overlooked in both the TASS dispatch and in the cablegram to U Thant.

The Red religious heads also claim: (1) to know what is 'Christian teaching' on the subject (no chapter or verse cited), and (2) to know the mind of God in regard to America's 'sin'.

The word 'peace', which has been abused and misused hundreds of times by the Communist propagandists since the close of World War II, is again dragged out, but this time with a religious trapping, to make the United States the villain and the USSR and Red Cuba the epitomes of sweetness and light.

O how often religion has been used as a convenient cover or "front" by scoundrels whose deeds of darkness and hypocrisy history has been bound to bring to light eventually!

The Russian Orthodox Church, the so-called All Union Council of Evangelical Christian Baptists, 'and others', are not genuine free religious groups or denominations such as we find in what remains of the Free World. They have become the most effective tools for the spread of Communist doctrines of any arm of the Soviet network. Thousands of documents and the testimonies of hundreds of exiled religious leaders and escapees from what was once Holy Mother Russia can be entered into the record under oath in any court of law or before any investigative committee of the United States Congress to prove the charge. This we must do in the pages which follow.

But, first we must turn to the record of history in order to understand the "how" and the "why" religious leaders can be used to spread the godless doctrines of Karl Marx, Frederich Engels, V. I. Lenin, Josef Stalin, Nikita Khrushchev and the present Soviet leaders.

A look of incredulity spreads over the face of the average church-goer in the United States when it is even suggested by the student of history that one garbed in religious regalia can be serving Satan while using godlike gestures and phraseology. So, the incredulity must be dispelled with hard cold facts, facts from sacred and secular history. To history we *must* turn at a time when the Red tide of Communism keeps flowing relentlessly on, engulfing even nations whose life has been steeped in centuries of religious activities and piety.

Not all which have borne the name "church" in the past have been necessarily the genuine House of Prayer. Not all who have taken or have had bestowed upon them religious titles have been the servants of God or of righteousness.

The "front" technique is as old as the Garden of Eden. It started with the first "covering up" act—fig leaves. Appearing to be something they were not, Adam and Eve thought they could hide their true identity.

The first systematic theologian of the Christian Church, the Apostle Paul, ripped off the mask of hypocrisy (putting on a front or disguise) from those who posed as "apostles of Christ" but who were revealed as "false apostles", "deceitful workers, transforming themselves into the apostles of Christ," and "ministers" of "Satan". (II Corinthians 11: 13-15)

When St. Paul was sitting in the prison house at Rome, waiting to be executed after many long years of preaching and defending the Christian faith, he wrote two final letters. Both were written to a young man whom Paul had discovered on one of his various missionary journeys and whom he had learned to love as a Christian son. Young Timothy was about to take up the battle where the great Apostle was to leave off.

In the first of these two letters the Apostle wrote a prophetic warning:

Now the Spirit (Holy Spirit) speaketh expressly, that in the latter times some shall depart from the faith, giving heed to seducing spirits, and *doctrines of devils* (emphasis added) ; speaking lies in hypocrisy; having their conscience seared with a hot iron. (I Timothy 4:1-2)

Here is the perfect description of the front technique. The Chinese call it "putting on a face" or a mask, as a character in disguise in a play. In other words, the real person is not seen because of the mask which covers him.

What better way to teach the devilish doctrines of Communism than to play the part of the religious hypocrite? Put on a religious "front" with all the regalia, symbols and rituals which go with it, and who is there who will dare challenge the authenticity of the fronter?

Another description which the Apostle Paul gave of the front technique is found in the Acts of the Apostles

narrative, Chapter 20, verses 27 through 31. In this passage
of church history Paul is recorded as having called the elders
of the Church of Ephesus together for a final farewell and
exhortation before he was to be taken captive to Rome and
suffer martyrdom. His words of warning to the Ephesian
Church overseers exactly parallel those spoken by Jesus
Christ, the head of the Church Universal, in Matthew's
Gospel, Chapter 7, verses 15 through 20.

In fact, Paul uses the same pastoral theme of sheep,
shepherd and wolves which Christ used in His warnings
concerning the front technique. Here are Paul's inspired
words:

> For I know this, that after my departing shall grievous
> wolves enter in among you, not sparing the flock. Also,
> of your own selves shall men arise, speaking perverse
> things, to draw away disciples after them. Therefore
> watch, and remember, that by the space of three years I
> ceased not to warn every one night and day with tears.
> (Acts 20:29-31)

Despite three years of day and night warnings, the
very things the Apostle Paul warned about, the infiltration
of the wolves, took place; and, history records that the
Church of Ephesus succumbed to the devilish doctrines of
the wolves and was soon buried by the sands of time.

Perversion or distortion of the truth is harder to detect
than an outright denial or falsehood. Error never rears
its ugly head in religious circles by identifying itself as
such. This would be too obvious to the members of the flock,
the sheep. So, again, it masters the "front" technique and
comes dressed in religious garb, as a sheep, but behind the
façade is the devouring and destroying wolf!

So it is with the modern technique used by the religious
front of the Soviet Union. Agents of the Kremlin, of the
dreaded Secret Police, the NKVD and KGB, present them-

selves to unsuspecting church-goers around the world as the genuine articles while all the time serving the godless Soviet state in the spreading of Communist poison ivy as green pasture to the unsuspecting sheep.

The names of Alexsei (often spelled "Aleksey" or "Alexei"), Sergei, Nikolai, Nikodim, Karpov, Zhidkov, Karev, Hromadka, Berecsky, Veto, Papp, and a host of other collaborators from the religious field with the Communist leaders are not in the vocabulary of the average church member in the Free World; yet, they are responsible for the spread of Communist propaganda around the world, the condemnation of the Western Powers and exhaltation of the Kremlin leaders while meeting with Western religious leaders and making pronouncments in their conferences, especially in the National and World Councils of Churches.

We will document their activities on behalf of the Communist Conspiracy in succeeding chapters of this book.

Let us now turn back the pages of history and then come forward to the present day. They have made the record. We did not make it for them. If they or their sympathizers object to us bringing the record out into the open, then they should never have made it. But as long as it is part of recorded history, we shall make it a point to bring it to the attention of people in the Free World far and wide. This is our responsibility as Christians. Once we have been warned and enlightened; once we have learned the irrefutable facts, it is our business, like an atomic chain reaction, to warn and to enlighten others, so that they in turn might reach others also. The freedom of the Free World hangs on such enlightenment. May it not be said in generations to come that we who knew the truth failed to convey it, like watchmen on the walls in the days of Ancient Israel, to those who depended upon our watchfulness for their security.

Chapter II
SOVIET CHURCH AND STATE

In the year 330 A. D. The Emperor Constantine changed the name of Byzantium to Constantinople and shifted the Roman Empire's throne to Constantinople, now known as Istanbul. Constantinople became known as the "second Rome" with the Patriarch of Constantinople becoming the rival of the Pope of Rome in both wealth and power.

Missionaries from Constantinople reached Russia in 998 A. D. Prince Vladimir was memorialized in statue in Kiev as the leading missionary who baptized the entire population of the city into the Eastern Orthodox faith.

The Great Schism, or split, between Constantinople and Rome took place in 1054 A. D. Eastern Orthodoxy traces its origin to the Holy Land where the first missionary work of the Early Church's apostles and evangelists began. Its main strength has always been in the Middle East, including parts of North Africa and Eastern Europe. It reached its great height in wealth and pomp under the Czars of Russia.

In 1500 A. D. autonomy was granted to the Russian section of the Orthodox church by the Patriarch of Constantinople. The Russian Church then elected its own Patriarch as ruler. Successive patriarchs ruled Russian Orthodoxy until 1721 when Czar Peter the Great established the Most Sacred Governing Synod to rule in place of the Patriarch.

For 400 years the church was aligned with the Russian government. It was supported by huge state subsidies which made it an ecclesiastical system unrivaled among the world's religions in power and wealth. A Chief Procurator was appointed by the Czar as a member of the Holy Synod "to protect and effectuate political interests." Practically all education was under the direction of the Russian Orthodox Church. The Czars were members of and patrons of the church.

Russian Orthodoxy even spread to the North American continent through missionaries who came to Russian-owned Alaska in the latter part of the 19th Century. The Diocese of Alaska and the Aleutians was created and later extended to include the United States and all of North America. The Moscow Patriarch was recognized as the ruler over this newly created diocese.

In 1917 the reign of the czars came to an end and the short-lived interim government headed by Alexander Kerensky took over. One of the first things which the Kerensky government did was to separate church and state. The Kerensky regime was not in favor with the hierarchy of the Russian Orthodox church because this separation stripped the church of a lot of its authority through the transferral of 37,000 schools—one third of all the schools in the land—to the control of the new Department of Education.

On October 30, 1917, while the Bolshevik revolution was in full swing and street fighting prevented many delegates from attending, the Russian Orthodox Sobor (official church conference), by a narrow vote of 141 to 112 restored the Patriarchate as the supreme ruler of the church, thus replacing the Most Sacred Governing Synod established by Czar Peter in 1721.

Three names were submitted in the Sobor for election to the office of Patriarch. Lots were cast by the delegates on November 18, 1917. The name of Tikhon was drawn from the urn by Hieromonk Alexei. Tikhon was enthroned as the head of the Russian Orthodox church around the world on 29 November 1917 in the Upensky Cathedral, despite the fact that the Kremlin was now completely in the hands of the Bolshevik revolutionists.

Scarcely were the ecclesiastical ceremonies concluded when active Communist persecution of the church began. The Bolsheviks sought to eliminate the church and its influence in the national life through killings and imprisonment of priests, bishops, nuns and monks. Thousands of houses of worship and monasteries were destroyed or were converted into stables for Red army horses, or into museums. By September 1923 the activity and the authority of the Patriarch of Moscow and All Russia had, for all purposes, ceased to exist.

Patriarch Tikhon brought the wrath of the Bolshevik regime down on his head shortly after his enthronement when he issued a pronouncement to the effect that the Communists would burn in Hell fire. He was marked for elimination by the Reds from then on.

The Bolshevik leaders had their helpers within the Russian Orthodox church. A group of disgruntled and ambitious radical priests created in December of 1922 a thing which became known as the Living Church Movement. Their idea was to capture control of the church machinery for themselves by internal subversion.

The Living Church Movement was based on the idea of reinterpreting the teachings of Christ and the Apostles in such a way as to serve Communist ends. For instance, there is a portion of the Bible which tells how Christ chased the moneychangers out of the temple. This would be interpreted that Christ was an anti-capitalist or against moneyed people! The general idea was to move from the spiritual concept to the materialistic one and to make the church an instrument of social strife, to substitute the materialistic social gospel for the supernatural salvation gospel.

The social gospel, which concentrates on all the so-called social problems that naturally could be exploited to create strife between classes, races, and different church groups, was the main device used to neutralize the anti-communist character of the church. Materialistic, humanistic and rationalistic philosophies were substituted for the divine historic message and mission of the church.

This movement lasted from 1918 to 1927. It received the active assistance of the Soviet Government and it succeeded in having Patriarch Tikhon deposed, tried and imprisoned. Although released from prison on June 25, 1923 after signing a so-called confession "acknowledging the correctness of the accusations" against him, he became quite broken in health and died on April 7, 1925.

The leaders of the Living Church Movement seized control of the Church administration in Moscow after the deposition of Tikhon, one of the factual conditions which led to the establishment of the Metropolitan District in the United States, separate from the Mother Church in Moscow.

The radicals in power set up their own Sobor in which:

1. They excoriated Tikhon as an "enemy of the state",

2. Expressed gratitude to the All-Russian Central Executive Committee for permission to convene,

3. Affirmed 'that every honorable Christian should take his place among these warriors for humanitarian truth' (meaning the Communists),

4. Urged the use of all means to realize in life the grand principles of the October Revolution (Bolshevik),

5. Declared that:

   (a) 'The Soviet power does not appear as a persecutor of the Church.'

   (b) 'The Constitution of the Soviet state provides full religious liberty.'

   (c) 'Church people must not see in the Soviet state a power of the anti-Christ.'

   (d) 'The Soviet power is the only one which attempts by state methods to realize the ideals of the Kingdom of God.'

   (e) Capitalism is the 'great lie' and a 'mortal sin',

   (f) The Soviet government is 'the world leader toward fraternity, equality, and international peace.'

How is that for a "non-political" church conference?

The Living Church Movement was eventually abandoned by the Soviet government because of the lack of popular support following the complete capitulation of Tikhon's successor, Sergei, to the Reds in 1927.

The Russian Orthodox Church has had only three patriarchs since the restoration of Tikhon to the throne in November of 1917: Tikhon, 1917-25; Sergei, 1943-44; and

Alexei, 1945—. Upon looking at these dates one is immediately inclined to raise the question of what happened to the
line of succession to the patriarchal throne between the
death of Tikhon in 1925 and the elevation of Sergei in 1943.

Twice Patriarch Tikhon had issued directives as to who
was to serve as *locum tenens* (temporary head) upon his
death until such a time as the Sobor could meet and elect
one of the three recommended successors. The reigning patriarch had always had the privilege of putting the names of
the three most qualified in his will. The Sobor then voted
on one of the three after the patriarch's demise.

Metropolitan Peter of Moscow took over the duties of
Guardian of the Patriarchal Throne but his term as temporary guardian was, indeed, exceedingly temporary. He was a
good man and a genuine non-political leader within the
church. However, the radicals of the Living Church Movement trumped up false charges against him, accusing him of
'counter-revolutionary activities abroad'. He was arrested by
the Secret Police (GPU) on December 10, 1925, sentenced
to exile within the USSR, and died in 1936. Two of the
three temporary substitutes for his office he had named while
serving in Moscow: Metropolitan Mikhail of the Ukraine and
Metropolitan Joseph of Rostov were arrested and exiled. This
left a third to be considered, Metropolitan Sergei of Nizhni
Novgorod, about whom we will have considerably more to
tell later.

At this point it should be mentioned that the North
American Diocese of the Russian Orthodox Church called
its own Sobor in Detroit, Michigan in 1924, and renounced
the jurisdiction of the Moscow hierarchy. Under the call of
Archbishop Platon of North America, the United States
group set up its own administration after it affirmed that the
Moscow patriarchate no longer was representative of the true
orthodox believers, but had rather become a tool of the

Communists. Moscow's reaction to this American move was violent, as we shall learn shortly.

As was mentioned previously, Tikhon's will named three possible successors to the Patriarchal Throne. Two were murdered after having been exiled. The third, one Sergei, emerged as *locum tenens,* or guardian of the throne in 1926. Sergei, too, was imprisoned, but then released in 1927 after he gave the Communist government his pledge of loyalty in behalf of the church in Russia and *abroad!*

Upon Sergei's capitulation to the godless Communist state, the Soviets then gave legal recognition to the Russian Orthodox Church, while not yet allowing a Sobor to be called for the election of Sergei to the Patriarchal Throne. That was to come much later. First, Sergei had to prove to the satisfaction of the Communist rulers that he could be completely depended upon to aid the cause of Communism.

Sergei went all out to please the Kremlin masters. One of the first things he did as temporary guardian of the throne was to write a letter in the form of an edict in which he demanded 'from the clergy abroad a written promise of their complete loyalty to the Soviet Government in all their public activities. Those who fail to make such a promise, or to observe it, shall be expelled from the ranks of the clergy subject to the Moscow Patriarchate.'

This capitulation by Sergei enabled him to act as *locum tenens* for the next 17 years, and finally to become Patriarch.

In 1927 Sergei had succeeded in registering himself and his temporary Holy Synod with the Soviet Government as the recognized administrator of the Church. The hierarchy had been practically outlawed since November of 1917. By his act, Sergei reestablished the link between church and state which had been broken during the regime of Alexander Kerensky; and, ironically enough, such reestablishment was not with a government which patronized and benevolently protected the church, such as under the Czars, but rather with a godless crowd of red atheists who had nothing but contempt for anything sacred, who slaughtered untold numbers of church leaders and worshippers, and who desecrated and demolished their houses of worship and study!

Sergei even hypocritically tried to reverse the facts of history in his fulsome praise of the Red regime. He declared the Soviet government guiltless of any wrongs done to the church and further stated that the Communist Government's 'distrust of all Church functionaries' was 'justified'. He and his successor, Alexei, have steadfastly maintained that there never was any persecution of religion in the USSR and no mention of any such has appeared in the official journals of the Moscow Patriarchate since Sergei's unholy capitulation to the unholy Communist State!

In 1934 Sergei issued a formal condemnation of the North American Metropolitan District which had been set up in Detroit in 1924, and which had refused to capitulate to Sergei's demands to bow the knee to the Red-cooperating Moscow hierarchy. Sergei's impudence in demanding, let alone expecting, defense of the Soviet government and loyalty to it by Orthodox Christians in the United States, was shocking beyond belief! Although he placed North American Bishop Platon under prohibition and sent one Fedchenkoff to the United States to take over, the U. S. Russian Orthodox Church ignored Sergei's orders and it continued to recognize Bishop Platon's authority. The Metropolitan District in North America grew and prospered despite Sergei's fulminations. The members were not about to pledge their loyalty to the Russian Communist rulers simply because their particular religious belief had been the dominant one in old Mother Russia for 400 years.

The New York State Court of Appeals, in rendering a decision on Russian Orthodox church property in New York City, which Moscow had been trying to seize control of from the local Cathedral of St. Nicholas, stated:

> The cataclysmic events in Russia following the Revolution there necessarily wrought profound change in the status, government, organization and administration of the Church. It is beyond doubt, that the "general" or central authority of this Church, the Moscow Patriarchate, persecuted as it was by the Communists, had ceased to exist as an operative and functioning entity by 1924.

The highest court of New York State said further in its decision against the Moscow group:

> The Patriarchate was subjected and subordinated to an anti-religious civil government. Sergei's capitulation, his so-called *modus vivendi* with the Communists, merely completed a process begun in 1918.

World War II brought even closer collaboration between the Russian Orthodox Church and the Communist State. Josef Stalin, master strategist for world conquest, came up with a brilliant idea for rallying the people of Russia together for defence of their homeland at a time when the Wehrmacht of Adolph Hitler was pressing deep into Soviet Territory.

Stalin watched with amazement as he saw Russian troops by the thousands and civilians by the hundreds of thousands deserting to the Nazi conquerors. Why was this happening? As the German forces penetrated Russian villages and cities, one of the first things they did was to reopen the churches and to restore imprisoned religious leaders to their pulpits, as the German Quartermaster Corps supplied them with vestments and liturgical articles.

Josef Vissarionovich got the point—fast!

He quickly summoned Sergei to a private conference within the Kremlin. Stalin told Sergei that if he would rally the masses of Russia together for a glorious defence of Holy Mother Russia, their sacred homeland, then he, Stalin, would grant great concessions to the churches.

Sergei wasted no time in fulfilling his part of the bargain. The marriage between the Church and the godless state was now consummated. He announced "prayers for our divinely protected land and its authorities, headed by its God-given leader," meaning, butcher Stalin.

"By its appeals to the people's patriotism the Church greatly aided the Kremlin in World War II. Now it is aiding the Kremlin in the cold war," writes Patricia Blake, veteran Moscow correspondent for *Life*.

"The Russian Church often acts as a handy mouthpiece for Soviet propaganda. In recent years it has attacked the Vatican, the United States, and various Western nations as warmongers, and it has called on all believers to participate in the Soviet-inspired Stockholm Peace Campaign," Miss Blake stated in September of 1959.

Miss Blake's mention of the Soviet-inspired Stockholm Peace Campaign, a petition-singing propaganda stunt, brings to mind that hundreds of liberal clergymen in the United States were caught in the trap as they gullibly signed this Moscow-originated plea.

Miss Blake further wrote, "The Korean War found the Patriarch of Moscow protesting to the U. N. Security Council against 'American Aggression.' 'The Russian Orthodox Church', wrote the Patriarch, 'decisively condemns this interference and the resulting annihilation of the peaceful population of Korea by American aviation.' "

This is mild compared to what the Foreign Secretary of

the Russian Orthodox Church had to say about the American Government and about the American GIs and officers in the Korean campaign. That story, however, must wait until we cover a few more preliminary pages of history.

Following the support rendered by the Moscow Patriarchate to the USSR during the invasion by Hitler, Josef Stalin permitted the Russian Orthodox Church to call a long-awaited Sobor in Moscow in September of 1943. On the eighth of September Sergei was elected by the hand-picked Kremlin-collaborating delegates as Patriarch of Moscow and All Russia.

There were some other interesting personages established in offices which did not require elections, however. One was Georgi G. Karpov who was given a seat on the SOVNARKOM (All Russian Council of Ministers—Politburo) as Minister of Church-State Affairs. No theological requirements were necessary to hold this position. He was well-qualified—a Major-General in the NKVD (Secret Police) who was to give orders to the Patriarch for transmittal down the religious chain of command. Stalin, himself, was well acquainted with this office as it was he, trained as a theological student, who held first this very same position in his climb up the Communist success ladder.

Karpov soon established 100 full-time branch offices of his department throughout all Russia in order to keep a fatherly eye on the doings of the religious arm of the Soviet Union. Helping him in this endeavor was one Comrade M. N. Pokrovsky who had the title of Head of the Department for Non-Orthodox Religious Bodies. He had a seat on the SOVNARKOM, also, from which he could keep an eye on the activities of the so-called "sects", such as Zhidkov's Baptists, Cheorekchayan's Armenians, Turs' Latvian Lutherans, Flavian's Old-Believers, Matsanov's Seventh-Day Adventists, Ghenchi's Calvinists, Khiyaletdinov's Muslems, Shiliffer and Shekhtman's Jews.

Sergei's reign was not for long. The second Patriarch of Russia (through the courtesy of Josef Vissarionovich Stalin) died 9 months after his elevation to the throne. It was May 15, 1944. The capitulation to the godless state, which Sergei had begun, was to go even deeper under his successor.

The brilliant church historian, Dr. Matthew Spinka, in his book THE CHURCH IN SOVIET RUSSIA (Oxford University Press, 1956) describes the results of Sergei's collaboration with the Communist government of Russia in these words:

> This then resulted in his ever-increasing subjection to governmental control, so that in the end but little actual difference could be discerned between the external relations vis-a-vis the Church which had existed under the Czarist regime and that which existed under the Soviets. It in turn established the pattern of relations which became not only the fixed form for Russia but for all communist-dominated countries as well. As such, this *modus vivendi*, whereby the Church has been lulled into the belief of the possibility of a 'peaceful co-existence' and of preservation of its essential rights, while in reality it has been used as a tool for eliminating all religion from society, presents perhaps the most difficult problem facing modern Christendom.

Metropolitan Alexei of Leningrad and Gorky was the obvious choice as Sergei's successor. On February 2, 1945, before the greatest pageantry and array of ecclesiastical dignitaries representing not only the new brand of Orthodoxy of the USSR, but also the Orthodoxy of Eastern Europe and the Middle East, the Sobor elected Alexei as Patriarch of what has been termed in Russia as 'Moscow-the-Third-Rome'. Even American delegates were invited to attend the Sobor but were prevented from arriving until after the election took place, because of the war.

Major General Karpov was there, not as a voting delegate! Such was reserved only for the clerics of the church, not for the State overseer! Something new was added to this ecclesiastical gathering. Karpov made a speech in which he praised the Russian Orthodox Church for its role in winning the war and then addressed the delegates on the relationship between Church and the Soviet state in which he reminded them that the Government was "supervising the correct and prompt execution of the laws and decrees of the government concerning the Russian Orthodox Church."

Also addressing the Sobor was one Nikolai Dorofeyevich Yarushevich, familiarly known to the assembly as Metropolitan of Moscow and Krutitse. Nikolai occupied a position in the Moscow Patriarchate under Sergei and Alexei second only to the Patriarchs themselves. He was actually the Foreign Secretary of the Russian Orthodox Church, or exporter of Communist propaganda to Orthodox and other religious groups inside and outside the Iron Curtain.

In his address Nikolai paid obeisance to General Karpov and to the Soviet Government by presenting a resolution expressing complete loyalty to the USSR which, under the watchful eye of Karpov, was unanimously passed!

The case history of Nikolai will be dealt with in complete detail in a separate chapter of this book.

Following his enthronement on February 4, 1945, Alexei and Karpov embraced and exchanged kisses three times publicly! The marriage between the Russian Orthodox Church and the State was now complete in every detail.

Dr. Spinka sums the relationship of the Church with the Soviet Government up in these words:

.. the state has been utilizing the Church as a tool for its own policies. Officially, it is claimed, of course, that Karpov's department in no way interferes with the autonomy of the Church's administration. But the instances of overt interferences are so numerous and incontrovertible that the claim is but another example of Soviet duplicity.

Patriarch Alexei made it clear that any reconciliation with groups in countries outside the USSR would have to be predicated on "the demand of the fullest loyalty; that is complete abstention from attacks on the Soviet Power is not political, but an ecclesiastical condition."

In regard to the North American Diocese which had renounced the Communist-controlled Moscow hierarchy's jurisdiction in 1924, Alexei imposed the requirement that in order to lift the spiritual separation from the Church in Russia it would have to pledge to abstain from political activities, which meant any criticisms of Communism or the Communist rulers. Further, the North American group would have to accept confirmation of an Archbishop to be appointed by Moscow to replace Platon's successor, Theophilus, who apparently was to be deposed.

The New York State Court of Appeals in its decision favoring the Cathedral of St. Nicholas in New York City as against the Moscow group said:

> If Sergei's acts as Patriarch may be considered equivocal with respect to his relationship with the Soviet, there is no doubt of vacillation in the policies of his successor and present head of the Russian Orthodox Church, Alexei. The famous church historian, Dr. Matthew Spinka of Hartford Theological Seminary has concluded that the fact remains that the Russian Church is subjugated by the state and exploited as a tool for the latter's far ranging policies.

The New York Court's conclusion can be proved by hundreds of most recent examples, some of which we will cite in these pages from time to time.

One of Alexei's first acts as Patriarch was to address a "love" letter to Josef Stalin. It was not addressed to him by his state title, that of Marshal Stalin, but rather in the chummy style of 'Dear Josef Vissarionovich':

> Our Orthodox Church has unexpectedly suffered a heavy trial: Patriarch Sergei, who has administered the Russian Church for eighteen years, has passed away.
>
> You well know with what wisdom he bore that laborious duty. You are acquainted with his love for the Fatherland, his patriotism which inspired him during the past war period. To us who were his closest collaborators, his feeling of the most sincere love and devotion to, as a wise, God-appointed Leader over the peoples of our great Union [that was his own actual expression] were well known. That feeling showed itself with unusual force after he had become personally acquainted with you on the fourth of September of the past year. Not a few times have I heard him recollect with tender feelings that meeting. He also attached high, historic significance to your regards for the needs of the Church, a regard most valuable to us.
>
> With his passing, our Church was orphaned. But, by the will of the late Patriarch, God has willed that I should take upon myself the duty of the Guardian of the patriarchate.
>
> In this most responsible moment of my life and my ministry in the Church, I feel the need to express to you, Dear Josef Vissarionovich, my personal feelings.
>
> In the task confronting me I will be steadfastly and inflexibly guided by the same principles which characterized the ecclesiastical career of the late Patriarch: on the one hand, I will adhere to the canons and regulations of the Church; and on the other, (I will adhere)

with steadfast loyalty to the Fatherland and to you as the head of its government.

Co-operating fully with the Council for the Affairs of the Russian Orthodox Church, and along with the Holy Synod established by the late Patriarch, I shall be protected against making mistakes and taking false steps.

I beg you, deeply honored and dear Josef Vissarionovich, to accept these assurances with the same good faith with which I make them, and to believe in my feelings of deep love and gratitude to you, by which all Church functionaries are inspired who are from henceforth to be guided by me.

The hypocrisy of Alexei, present ruler of the Russian Orthodox Church, is seen in every paragraph of the letter. For him to attribute the appointment of Stalin over the peoples of Russia to the Almighty God is not only hypocrisy of the sheerest kind but also downright blasphemy! Shades of the millions of slaughtered Christians and followers of other faiths who were executed on orders of this so-called 'God-appointed leader' who had nothing but contempt for anything God-like or sacred! Who could believe that God selected Stalin to rule Russia so that he might destroy the Houses of God and blaspheme His name?

How could Sergei have had 'tender feelings' over a meeting with the Red Butcher of the Kremlin when, after all, Stalin ordered Sergei to appear at the meeting in which Stalin revealed his diabolical plan for using the Russian Church to save his own hide from defeat by the forces of Adolph Hitler? What 'regards for the needs of the Church' had Stalin shown prior to the historic meeting with Sergei? How could Alexei be steadfastly 'loyal' to Stalin's regime and to the Church at the same time? Perhaps the explanation is that nowhere in the letter did Alexei say that he would be loyal to Christ, the true head of the Church, or to

God's holy word, the Bible. With the Russian Church now
being run from top to bottom by Communists, Secret Police
agents, and collaborators with Communists, it was perfectly
in order for Alexei to say that he could be loyal to the
godless Red regime of the USSR and to the Red-run Church
at the same time!

The most ironical part of Alexei's epistle is that he
tells 'Dear Josef' what 'Dear Josef' already knows too well:
that he, Alexei, will cooperate 'fully' with Karpov's administration of Church affairs and that he 'shall be protected
against making mistakes and taking false steps'.

What better 'protection' against making mistakes could
Alexei have than the watchful eyes of a Major General of
the Soviet Secret Police, Karpov?

Alexei's expression of 'love and gratitude' to Josef Stalin
shows the unmistakable depths to which wolves in sheep's
clothing, as Jesus Christ and the Apostle Paul said, can
descend. Surely the blood of Russian martyrs, clergy and laity
alike, must have cried aloud from Russian and Satellite soil
in vehement protest over this demagoguery!

This letter, written shortly after his ascension to the
Russian Orthodox throne shows beyond question upon what
course Alexei would steer the Russia Orthodox Church. The
Church would be an arm of the Soviet Propaganda machine
while maintaining a religious façade. Time would soon prove
that the Russian Orthodox Church was to become one of the
most effective instruments for the spread of Communist
doctrines around the world which was ever devised by the
rulers of the Kremlin.

If Alexei's tributes to Josef Stalin were fulsome hypocrisy, those of his Second in Command, Comrade Metropolitan Nikolai of Moscow, Foreign Secretary of the Church,
consisted of rapturous praise.

Upon the celebration of the twenty-sixth anniversary of the bloody Bolshevik revolution, Nikolai penned for the Journal of the Moscow Patriarchate, official proceedings of the Russian Orthodox Church printed every thirty days and received in the U. S. Library of Congress, an article which is revealing in its tribute to Stalin:

> Our Church members, along with the entire population, discern in our Leader [Stalin] the greatest (man) that has ever been born in our country. For he unites in his person all the characteristics mentioned above in connection with our Russian bogatyrs [great heroes] and the great military leaders of the past. Our people see in him the incarnation of all that is best and brightest; all which represents the holiest heritage of our Russian nation bequeathed to us by our ancestors. In him are indissolubly united the fervent love of the Fatherland and of the nation, the most profound wisdom, the strength of a manly and firm spirit, and a fatherly heart. . .
>
> The name of Josef Vissarionovich Stalin, surrounded by the deepest love of all nations of our country, is the banner of glory, culture, and greatness of our Fatherland!

A summary of Foreign Secretary Nikolai's tribute to Stalin could read like this:

1. Number one candidate for Father of the Year.
2. Greatest man ever born.
3. All the population of Russia (no polls taken!) agree on his greatness.
4. An incarnate shining example of moral virtue.
5. The holiest of holy men of all times.
6. The fountain of wisdom, itself.
7. Number one Russian Patriot.
8. Male matinee idol of all time.
9. The banner of glory, culture and greatness to inspire unprecedented flag-waving!

One wonders how silly Russian Church leaders can get. What denials or withdrawals of this nonsensical adoration of the Red Butcher did Nikolai make after Khrushchev took over and de-Stalinized Stalin, making him out to be a scoundrel of the lowest degree, a liar, a butcher, a hypocrite, and not worthy of a place even in the mausoleum in Red Square? What virture was there in a man who had his first wife murdered?

The silence of Alexei, Nikolai and Company was deafening!

The New York State Court of Appeals gave an excellent description of Alexei and his collaboration with the Communist state:

Patriarch Alexei has always appeared to be an ardent supporter of the Soviet State. He was an outspoken admirer of Stalin, whom he pledged unswerving loyalty. The proceedings of the 1945 Sobor which elected him read more like a Communist party rally than the solemn conclave of a major religious faith. He and his official publications, such as the monthly Journal of the Moscow Patriarchate, received by the U. S. Library of Congress, have warmly supported the standard Communist "line" on various political matters. At appointed times, he and the Orthodox Church have sponsored or supported so-called "Peace Conferences" extolling Russia and condemning the West. The Journals of the Moscow Patriarchate, which have on occasions been excluded from the United States mails on the ground of constituting political propaganda, are replete with virulent and intemperate false attacks upon the government, people and policies of the United States. Every area of political conflict between the United States and Russia becomes the subject of another tirade, more vicious and more effective for the very reason that it appears in a church publication, under ecclesiastical sanction, and couched in phrases borrowed from the religious lexicon. Thus, the

United States has been castigated by Alexei's church as "the fornicatrix of the resurrected Babylon," "the Washington Cain," "the Beast of the Apocalypse" and "the contemporary blood-thirsty Baal."

Very accurately did the New York Court speak. But half has not been told. All the base lies of Soviet propaganda regarding alleged American germ warfare and mass rape in Korea to imperialist and warmongering designs in the Middle East and in Cuba are duly and faithfully parrotted by the Russian Orthodox Church journals.

The Moscow Patriarchate has declared:

The great blasphemy from the Christian point of view is the fact that these American people call themselves Christians.

Chapter III
COMRADE NIKOLAI

As stated before, the entire case history of the propaganda utterances of the Foreign Secretary of the Russian Orthodox Church, Comrade Nikolai Dorofeyavich Yarushevich, Metropolitan of Moscow and Krutitse, now deceased, needs to be set forth so that every church member in what remains of the Free World can profit by the unmasking of one of the worst wolves in sheep's clothing of modern times.

Although written nearly six hundred years ago Chaucer's observation that "murder will out" still holds good today. *The New York Times* for June 9, 1956 carried a news photo showing the Rev. Eugene Carson Blake, President of the National Council of Churches, escorting Metropolitan Nikolai of Russia to visit Independence Hall in Philadelphia. The picture shows a solid line of police holding back angry demonstrators shouting epithets at the Soviet clergyman. Some of them probably shouted "murderer" at the holy man from Russia. Millions of Americans no doubt were shocked at such rudeness and incivility.

Page 114 of *LIFE* for March 23, 1959 again shows Metropolitan Nikolai this time officially branded as a Soviet secret agent by a high ranking Soviet Secret Police official, Petr Deriabin, who defected to the West. Between these two pictures hangs a tale—a tale of consummate villainy and cynical fraud beyond all historical parallel.

In March, 1956, nine prominent leaders of the NCC headed by Eugene Carson Blake journeyed to Moscow at the invitation of the Soviet government through Metropolitan Nikolai, second ranking Orthodox hierarch in all of the USSR. The NCC leaders came back bursting with enthusiasm and praise for Metropolitan Nikolai. They did not have much to say about just who this Soviet clergyman was and what his background might be. Soviet Russia is a land of mystery and secrecy and it is often very hard to dig out even the most elementary facts readily available to anyone in a non-Communist country.

Metropolitan Nikolai of Krutitse and Kolomna, to give his full title, was born Boris Dorofeyevich Yarushevich, in Kovno in 1891. His father was an arch-priest in the old Russian Orthodox Church. Young Yarushevich became a monk in 1914. He was graduated from a theological seminary a year later.

On November 7, 1917, Lenin's Bolsheviki stormed the Winter Palace in Petrograd and overthrew the liberal democratic government of Kerensky. Within three months the Bolsheviks began the destruction of religion in Russia. It is highly significant that the victorious Bolsheviks struck at religion long before they began their expropriation of all property and other assaults on human freedom and dignity. Mark well the date because this is highly important in our study of the rise of Metropolitan Nikolai.

Shuster in his very important and scholarly "Religion Behind the Iron Curtain" states:

> The Communists attacked with blind fury. Church property was taken away, priests were left without any means of subsistence. Houses of worship were profaned. A few excerpts from the pastoral letter issued by Patriarch Tikhon on January 18, 1918, summarize the situation at that time:
>
> 'Daily we are in receipt of letters reporting the horrible, bestial murders of quite innocent and bed-ridden people .... There are no hearings, all rights and laws have been abrogated. The holy edifices are targets for gunfire, or are subjected to looting, ridicule and degradation. Venerable persons residing in monasteries and honored by the faithful are seized by the dark, ungodly powers of this age. Schools supported by the Orthodox Church for the education of priests are turned into institutions of non-believers or are made into houses of prostitution.'
>
> The Metropolitan of St. Petersburg, the Metropolitan of Kiev, and the chief representative of the Roman Catholic Church in Russia were tried and executed. How many others suffered a like fate, no one knows.

We now know that thousands of priests, monks, and other religious leaders were horribly murdered or exiled to slow death in Siberia. Churches were despoiled, robbed of their valuable ikons and other wealth and converted into granaries, barracks or even stables.

And while all this was going on how fared our "dearly beloved brother" Metropolitan Nikolai, bosom friend of Eugene Carson Blake and other American modernist, ecumenical, leftwing clergymen?

In 1918 Boris Yarushevich, while churches were being closed and desecrated all over Russia, became head of the Peter and Paul Cathedral in Peterhof. The next year he became Archimandrite and head of the Alexander Nevsky

Monastery of Petrograd. In 1922 he became Bishop of Peterhof and Petrograd diocese. That same year a priest named Vvedensky started the "Living Church" movement which enjoyed the official protection and approval of the Bolshevik regime.

The supreme head of the Orthodox Church, Patriarch Tikhon was arrested in July 1922. He died three years later. From 1925 to 1943 no election of a new Patriarch was permitted by the Soviets. Indeed, the very title disappeared from all official documents and from the press. It was forbidden to use any religious title in any publication. The death of Patriarch Tikhon was merely announced as that of "Citizen" Belavin.

Before his death Tikhon had designated Metropolitan Cyril as keeper of his office. Orthodox canon law empowered only a Sobor or general council of top hierarchs as guarding the ecclesiastical succession. The Soviet government immediately arrested Cyril. Tikhon's second choice had been Metropolitan Agaphangel but he was already in exile. Patriarch Tikhon's third choice was Metropolitan Peter but he was arrested as soon as he assumed office and transported to Siberia where he died in 1936.

With the death of Metropolitan Peter the legitimate succession of ecclesiastical authority was wiped out forever. Out of eleven hierarchs appointed to act as keeper or deputy ten died in exile or in prison. The present Patriarch, like Metropolitan Nikolai, is nothing more than a Secret Police appointee and hence devoid of any bona fide ecclesiastical authority.

In 1936 Nikolai had advanced under the soviet Secret Police to Archbishop of Peterhof and Novgorod diocese. In 1939 he was Exarch of the Ukraine. While Khrushchev was busy purging the Communist Party of the Ukraine his henchman Nikolai directed a merciless campaign of persecution against the Ukrainian Orthodox Autocephalous Church as well as against the Greek Catholics and Ukrainian Roman Catholics. Hundreds of priests and thousands of laymen were deported to slave labor camps and a more or less speedy death.

In 1942 Nikolai made the news in Russia by being the first religious leader since the 1917 Revolution to be officially recognized by title in an official Soviet document. He was appointed a member of a Commission to Investigate German Atrocities. As this was fully a year before Stalin deigned to take official notice of Nikolai's superior, Patriarch Sergius, it must be quite obvious who the favorite boy of the Bolsheviks was. Sergius was also restored to some limited degree of authority and prestige as part of the Communists' use of religion to bolster sagging Soviet morale under the hammer blows of Hitler's onsweeping Reichswehr.

With the end of World War II Metropolitan Nikolai's real role in Soviet foreign policy began to unfold itself— that of an international Judas leading the innocent faithful into the Red abbatoir of nations and peoples. In 1945 he was the directing genius of the Moscow Sobor which arbitrarily brought the Orthodox churches of newly conquered satellites under the Moscow Patriarchate. Metropolitan Nikolai began to travel extensively and frequently in western Europe building up contacts with various Protestant denominations. In 1948 he was busy in Stockholm with the phony Stockholm Peace Appeal.

On February 23, 1951 the Communist World Council of Peace met in East Berlin, Germany. A featured speaker at the Red gathering was Metropolitan Nikolai of Moscow. This agent of KGB (successor to the NKVD, Soviet Secret Police) launched a vitriolic attack against the United States. Here are some of the vicious charges made by this so-called "Christian" leader of the Soviet Orthodox Church who fraternized with leaders of the National and World Councils of Churches, and who joined them in the World Council:

We all know how on June 25, 1950, the hordes of the Korean American marionette—Li Sun Man, villainously fell upon the Peoples-Democratic Korean Republic, at the direction of their American masters. The pains-taking elaboration of this act, horrible in its baseness, is known.

It is known how the freedom-loving Korean people answered the bloody attack in one outburst. It is known how President Truman gave the order to the American armed forces in the Far East to come to the aid of his true ally—Li Sun Man.

It is known by what methods the United States of America influenced and (what methods it) uses to put through the UN resolutions it desires.

The demogogic wails of American propagandists are known, with which they try to cover up the bestial grin of imperialism revealed to the whole world.

The march of military actions on the fronts of this long-suffering land is known. The boundless courage and heroism, with which an ancient people defends its independence and life before the hordes of contemporary savages, is known. What sympathy and condolence are called forth by the sufferings of the Korean people from all freedom-loving humanity, are known.

And there is also known one circumstance of the Korean events, and it is to this circumstance that I want to draw your attention. I have in mind the conduct of the war in Korea by the American aggressors.

When we turn to the official statements of the governmental workers of the Korean Peoples-Democratic Republic; when we listen to the evidence of war correspondents, journalists, up to now not known for the progressiveness of their opinions; when living people speak, who by some miracle have survived after the retreat of the army of occupation, or those who managed to escape from the leprous regions of the "new Americanized order"—we feel that which no document can transmit: we feel that depth of boundless, unassuageable grief into which modernized American monsters have plunged a noble people with its ancient culture.

And so we become convinced that the spirit and substance of fascism have not disappeared, that the delirious dreams of the fanatic Hitler have found their continuers, now trying to realize them.

Their followers do not lag behind their teachers.

From the first day of the lawless aggression the American neofascists began a systematic cannibalistic destruction of the "lower" Korean race.

What do we see?

Cynically violated standards not only of international rights, but of human morals. Executions without trial and inquisitions, secret and public. Dreadful tortures of victims; the cutting off of ears and noses, breasts, the putting out of eyes, the breaking of arms and legs, the crucifixion of patriots, the burial alive in communal graves of women with children at their breasts, etc. The rebirth of the customs of savages—the scalping of Korean patriots for "souvenirs."

For the purposes of annihilating the population, the American criminals first of all fanatically killed the political prisoners (from 200,000 to 400,000 persons), forcing them first to dig their own graves; they threw the bodies of patriots (who had been) hung, shot or who died from typhus into a precipice and, to conceal the traces, blew up a cliff above it.

The barbaric bombings of peaceful cities and centers of population were directed exclusively toward the annihilation of the civil population.

In the committees of inquiry of the American troops we see the reborn "technique" of Hitler, inhuman tortures of Korean patriots; hanging by the hands, binding (them) behind the back, which is impudently called "aeroplane"; welding handcuffs on the hands behind the back for 2-3 months; torture by electricity, including the electric bed, on which death follows the transmission of a strong current; a wet leather jacket which crushes the breast of the victim on drying; placing those ill of an epidemic sickness in cells filled to overflowing with prisoners.

These civilized savages arranged shooting matches with living targets, binding peasants to posts with barbed wire and shooting each of them over the heart of the target. Reviving the customs of the young-fascists, young-yankees photographed these scenes for their family albums and sent them home to their fiancees and wives. These representatives of the "higher" race practised and practice mass rape of the women and young girls of Korea, rounding them up from surrounding towns, making them drunk on gin and raping them. Not limited to outrages, the miserable victims were driven, in places, into tunnels, shot by machine-guns and buried under the debris of blown up cliffs.

Often one can see on the roads of Korea the still warm corpse of a mother and a crying child at her breast. Cases are known when children, born in prison, were trampled by the soldiers boots in front of the mother, and then the mother was killed.

On retreating, this "flower of culture" destroyed or drove off with it all living things on the evacuated lands. On attacking, their fury was also vented first of all on the peaceful people.

Thus, on landing on September 15 in the Bay of Inchon everything breathing in the region was annihilated by insane forty-eight hour fire. Upon attacking Seoul in September of 1950 the same tactics of general destruction was continued.

In September of 1950, the French journalist Charles Farvel visited the camp of death, located in the "Valley of Horror" in Southern Korea. More than 300,000 Koreans are doomed to death in that camp. At that time there were 10 such camps. The camps are surrounded by barbed wire, along which run high voltage electric currents. The people live on the ground, they have neither clothing nor shoes. They are not fed, they eat grass and the bark of trees and bushes. American scientists and doctors, under the guise of giving medical assistance, test the newest vaccines and chemical preparations on the prisoners. Every night there are executions in the ravines surrounding the camps. To be destroyed in the first order are the intelligentsia of the Korean people: doctros, teachers, engineers, technicians, agriculturists.

"I accuse!"—declared the Korean artist (a woman) Zoe Sin Hee—"The blood of thousands of infants, destroyed by the Americans, the tens of thousands tortured in the camps of death, the hundreds of thousands killed at the front, call for justice. The American military criminals must be severely punished for their evil deeds. I accuse them. I believe that the hour of retribution will soon arrive."

In retreating in January of 1951, the occupation forcibly chased more than two million peaceful inhabitants to the south of Korea, who died in thousands on the road and the roadside ditches from hunger and cold, from the bullets of aggressors.

Those of the peaceful population of Northern Korea who remained alive or were dispersed among the camps expected hunger and epidemics. Even the notorious "UN Commission on the Unification and Re-establishment of Korea" in its letter to the UN of February 1, 1951, notes that 3,628 Koreans have been left without a roof in penury.

The Korean children are everywhere subject to the fury of the occupation. Everywhere, where the foot of the interveners has stepped—in the province of Southern Pennyan, Northern Kengke, Southern Kengke, Kanko, Chang-Bong—the American bandits have destroyed the children.

And again one cannot dismiss the thought that the ideologists guiding the dreadful events in Korea consider themselves to be Christians, and not only Christians, but even leaders of Christian organizations! They know the Bible and often state so in the hearing of all!

And reason refuses to give an explanation of this nightmare, and the heart does not cease to tremble from feelings of holy hatred toward the cannibals, and the conscience of all simple people cries out against the evil deeds of the American aggressor!

Waves of protest and indignation against the American aggressor in Korea and the evil deeds of the occupation; against the attempts to loosen a new world war by means of blocs, pacts, the remilitarization of Germany and Japan; against the exploitation of the UN by the United States of America as a weapon of aggression—roll over the entire world. This indignation against the rulers who have lost their reason and will, dragging people towards the precipice, can be heard in numberless petitions, sent to parliaments and ministries. It is heard in the appearances of women and young people, going on in all the countries of the world. Protest and indignation is expressed by the many-thousand-strong crowds gathering in the town squares of Europe and demanding that the oversea world bandits and world colonizers in dresscoats and generals' tunics return home.

And our holy duty, dear friends is to tighten our ranks in the fight for peace, for the cessation of the bloody aggression in Korea, in the fight against the remilitarization of Western Germany and Japan, as a step towards a new war, against weapons for the mass annihilation of people, for the progressive curtailing of armament.

Nikolai's atrocity story varies a bit from the official North Korean version which charged the American soldiers buried young Korean children alive with only their heads sticking above the ground and then used these live baby heads as targets for routine rifle practice.

In December that same year Nikolai charged that:

American aggressors continue to wage a war of extermination in Korea. . . . The ideas of hatred of humanity are innoculated in children and young people on a broad scale in the U.S.A. It is thus that the American kindlers of war try to raise murderers from their tender years.

In 1952 Metropolitan Nikolai charged that U. S. airmen in Korea were waging germ warfare:

Infected insects are being dropped from American aircraft on populated points, not only in Korea but in China . . . . The church cannot pass over in silence the sufferings of the Korean people, which is perishing from the brigandlike attack and demoniac malice of these human monsters. We shall hope that the Lord will put to shame the modern bloodthirsty Baal attempting to catch the entire world in his net, that the dread hand of Providence will restore the truth that has been defiled.

Nikolai did not think much better of Pope Pius XII whom he regarded as a mere "agent of American imperialism."

These are but a few brief excerpts from pages of similar slanders by Metropolitan Nikolai which have appeared in the Soviet press and journals.

At this point the sceptic will probably ask: "Why should the atheist Soviet regime build up religion when its own history and all its official pronouncements decree the death of all religions under the sickle and hammer?" With a cynicism without parallel in history, the Communists use the Russian Orthodox Church as a weapon for world domination and the ultimate extinction of all religious belief.

By re-establishing and granting quasi-recognition to the church, the atheistic and cynical Russian Communists have accomplished the following:

1. Enabled them to assimilate and to bring under their control the Orthodox churches of the conquered satellites of East Europe.

2. Helped toward an old Russian objective—to make Moscow the "Third Rome".

3. Hampered the spread of the underground or catacomb church.

4. Gave the Soviets enormous world-wide prestige as many religious people, impressed by the apparent restoration of the Orthodox Church, lessened their suspicion of and animosity towards the Soviet Union. An apparently free functioning hierarchy and "packed Churches" were witness to the liberality and tolerance of the Soviets towards organized religion.

5. With secret police agents posing as priests and listening to confessions, as well as penetrating every strata of the hierarchy, it gave the Soviet police state another secret observation post inside the minds of the enslaved Russian people.

6. Enabled venal and treacherous Soviet clergymen to build bridges of contact and confidence with western clergymen and in turn rope them in on all manner of Soviet propaganda enterprises; viz. the Stockholm Peace Appeal, World Congresses for Peace, etc.

7. Enabled the Soviet government through its religious stooges to by-pass the Ecumenical Patriarch of Constantinople and the Roman Catholic Church and deal directly with other Christian denominations throughout the non-Communist world.

For example, in July, 1948, the Moscow Conference of the heads and representatives of the Orthodox Autocephalous

Churches announced that universal Christianity was not identified with western civilization; that most western Christian sects no longer followed the precepts of Christ and the True Faith and were sunken in materialism, greed, vice, and corruption. Only the Orthodox Church represented the True Faith and Communism was nothing more than the Kingdom of God on this earth. Nine months later the First World Congress of Peace Partisans meeting in Paris issued a manifesto embracing much the same general line—that the West had abandoned Christianity in its mad search for ever greater nuclear bombs and mass destruction weapons.

The Soviet hierarchy therefore have become an extremely valuable and important weapon in the arsenal of world Communism as directed from Moscow. And, Metropolitan Nikolai of Krutitse and Kolomna has been one of the most important front men in this international confidence game to bamboozle gullible western clergymen into acting as dupes for all sorts of Communist propaganda swindles and confidence games!

If your church adheres to the National Council of Churches and the World Council you officially have been associated with Boris Dorofeyevich Yarushevich, alias "Metropolitan Nikolai" in this most colossal and cynical hoax. Take another look at page 11f of March 23, 1959 issue of *LIFE* and read Mr. Deriabin's sensational article.

The NCC's *Outlook* for May, 1956, in defending the Moscow visit of nine of its top leaders commented, "Only a few seem to think it wrong for American Christians to talk with Russian Christians." The testimony of Soviet defector Deriabin can now leave no doubt that the Rev. Eugene Blake and his associates were not talking to "Russian Christians" at all but to Soviet secret police agents and their stooges masquerading in clergymen's clothes.

Thus, official Soviet sources leave no doubt that Nikolai rose steadily to the second top ecclesiastical post in all of Russia while the Bolsheviks were exterminating the rest of the Orthodox clergy and extirpating all religions. As priests were murdered or deported to slow deaths in Siberia Nikolai stepped from one sacerdotal preference to the next. When Khrushchev went to the Ukraine to wipe out all anti-Soviets in blood purges, Metropolitan Nikolai was on hand to handle the purges of the clergy.

Metropolitan Nikolai's blood-strewn trail is a matter of open record in official Soviet documents. This record was available to the Rev. Eugene Carson Blake and his National Council of Churches' associates when they went to Russia in 1956 and subsequently invited Nikolai to this country. The Deriabin disclosure merely confirms and clinches the record.

In October of 1956 when the Soviet armed might crushed the uprising of the Hungarian people who were fighting for their freedom, National and World Council of Churches leaders from the United States frantically sent cables to Metropolitan Nikolai asking him to use his influence to stop "the bloodshed and oppression in Hungary". This is the same Nikolai with whom they had been doing business for years, while wooing the Russian Orthodox Church into the fold of the World Council.

Nikolai sent a hypocritical reply saying, "Our Government (the USSR) is giving *material* aid to those who suffer in Hungary and we shall devotedly and unceasingly labor for peace".

The "material aid" seemed to be in the form of tanks, mortars, rifle and machine gun fire which shattered Budapest, setting hospitals afire with hundreds of the helpless cremated in their beds, and the mowing down of thousands of patriotic young people who fought with their bare fists, homemade

Molotov cocktails, and other improvised weapons in defence of their homeland.

No word of criticism of the Soviet Union has ever been uttered publicly by Nikolai, Alexei or other leaders of religion in the Soviet Union. Although Nikolai had ample opportunity to tell the truth when he came to the United States as a guest of Dr. Eugene Carson Blake and the National Council of Churches he continued to use his ecclesiastical office as a mouthpiece from which to spout more Russian-style "peace" propaganda before many gullible American churchmen who had never done their "homework".

On October 15, 1955 the Communist Hungarian Church Press announced that Metropolitan Nikolai of Russia had received the Soviet Union's Red Flag Order of Work. Hungarian Communist Bishop Albert Bereczsky sent his congratulations!

In a letter to *The New York Times,* Dated June 5, 1956, Nicholas D. Chubaty, author and former Professor of East European History, now editor of *The Ukranian Quarterly,* charged Nikolai with promoting religious persecution in the Ukraine. Here is Professor Chubaty's letter:

To the Editor of the New York Times:

An ecclesiastical delegation headed by Metropolitan Nikolai has arrived in the United States as guests.

It has already been mentioned in the press that Metropolitan Nikolai, de facto Vice Regent of the Moscow Patriarchate, is the real promoter of all its church and political policy. He is the liaison between the Russian Orthodox Church and the Soviet Government, the clergyman most favored by the Kremlin.

Some facts of his activity are less known to the American people. Metropolitan Nikolai is an active promoter of the religious persecutions in the Ukraine of the Orthodox adherents as well as the Greek Catholics.

He presecuted the Ukrainian Orthodox Autocephalous Church by trying Metropolitan Polykarp in absentia before the church court in Moscow. He then issued a proclamation which was full of distortions and slanders on the Ukrainian Orthodoxes who favored autocephaly. This proclamation was a guide for the terroristic action of the MVD against the Ukrainian Orthodox Church when the Red Army in 1944 again started to occupy the Ukraine. Metropolitan Nikolai became expert in Ukrainian church affairs for the Moscow Patriarchate.

Destruction of Church

But a totally un-Christian persecution was started in 1945 against the Ukrainian Greek Catholics in the western provinces of the Ukraine, in Galicia and Carpatho-Ukraine, occupied by the Soviets. This church of over four million followers was condemned to destruction by fire and sword. In this barbaric action we see the harmonious cooperation between the Moscow Patriarchate and the Soviet police.

In April, 1945, in one day in Soviet-occupied Galicia were imprisoned all five Ukrainian Catholic Hierarchs. Simultaneously a group of three renegade clergy was created to liquidate the Ukrainian Catholic Church and bring it under the Russian Orthodox Patriarchate in Moscow.

In May, 1945, the Moscow Patriarch issued a proclamation to the Catholic Ukrainians of this part of the country to abandon the Catholic Church and join the Russian Orthodoxy. The appeal was entirely without results because here the Catholic Church was closely connected with the entire national life.

Denunciation of Dissidents

When the Patriarch's voice sounded in the wilderness the Soviet Government came to his assistance, in spite of the separation between church and state. The Klevan Police Department under the signature of one Khodchanko in June, 1945, issued an official decision approving the committee of three renegade priests as the church authority for Ukrainian Catholics in Galicia, demanding registration of all the dissidents and their denunciation to the M.V.D.

In June, 1945, in the St. George Cathedral in Lvov, the sanctuary of the Greek Catholic Ukrainians, a meeting of over three hundred priests was held. Quoting the Stalin constitutions on the freedom of religion and of the separation of church and state, they composed a memorandum to the Moscow Government asking the release of the imprisoned Bishops. All 300 courageous priests were arrested.

The treatment in the prison of Metropolitan Joseph Slipy, the Primate and prominent scholar, was most brutal.

The Moscow Patriarchate after removal of the Catholic hierarchy from Western Ukraine with the help of the M.V.D. called a mock synod in St. George Cathedral in Lvov composed of 204 priests and twelve laymen assembled with the support of Soviet authorities. They proclaimed the separation of the Ukrainian Catholic Church from Rome and dependency from Moscow. The synod was ignored by Western Ukrainians of Galicia, whose church went underground. Hundreds of priests and thousands of the faithful were deported to the concentration camps as martyrs for the faith.

Nicholas D. Chubaty.

New York, June 5, 1956

Chapter IV

PATRIARCHAL POWER

Patriarch Alexei also issued a statement on the Hungarian situation:

> When the fate of Hungary hung in the balance, Orthodox Christians in our country prayed for a speedy end to the bloodshed. In certain foreign circles a quite different attitude was taken at the time: promising the counter-revolutionary rebels (*notice how he designates the Hungarian Freedom Fighters*) help from the West, these circles made every effort to inflame hostilities and to make disorder in Hungary, calculating to turn her against the Soviet Union and to kindle the flames of a third world war. But that plan happily did not succeed and the Christians of the East and West again faced the necessity of combining their efforts with the aim of pacifying the peoples.

Here is certainly the epitome of satanic hypocrisy on the part of the head of the Russian Orthodox Church. He attacks those of the Free World who wanted aid sent to the struggling Hungarian people who in turn desired only their freedom from Soviet oppressors, help which, of course, never came from the West whose leaders were rendered immobile by the successful Soviet propaganda of the type written by Alexei, namely: we can't aid the forces of freedom anywhere in their struggle against Soviet Communism because such aid might bring on a third world war or the nuclear destruction of civilization. How triumphant the Communists have become over this clever ruse to stymie aid for people who want their freedom. The Reds march on and take more of the world, piece by piece, by internal subversion and by supplying puppet leaders and forces with the weapons of war in order to keep the masses who want their freedom in subjection. The West trembles before the threat of nuclear war and seems to say in so many words, "We cannot afford to send help to the Hungarians or to the Cubans, because the Soviets might unleash a nuclear attack and bring on a third world war which will destroy humanity, and we would then be responsible for pushing the button which started it all."

The Soviet clerics know the weaknesses of the West so well that they have been laughing up their ecclesiastical sleeves at us, while mouthing "peace" slogans on behalf of the advancing Communist forces and holding religious "peace" conferences in which the United States, England, West Germany and other free nations are denounced for disturbing the peace of the world.

In the St. Nicholas Cathedral versus the Moscow group case, the New York State Court of Appeals ruling had a great deal to say about the use of Alexei and his henchmen by the Kremlin in advancing the Communist cause:

> We have seen that Alexei was elected Patriarch of Moscow at the Sobor of 1945 succeeding Sergei who had died. It is a matter of history that when the Soviets were fighting for survival during the World War, and in view of the defections by the populace to the German invaders who had opened the churches and proclaimed freedom

of worship, Stalin granted concessions to Sergei and received in return the patriotic support of the Patriarchate throughout the war. The Patriarchate was permitted to exist and function on a limited scale in return for some service which it might render to the Soviet State. What we see is a picture of the Church and its leaders permitted a nominal existence and observance of religious rites within Russia on a narrow scale. There is overwhelming and conclusive evidence that this nominal existence and the performance of these rites are permitted by the Soviet Government simply as a matter of expediency, that the Patriarchate either willingly or as a price of survival serves the aims, purpose and objectives of the Soviet Government at home and *abroad* [emphasis added] and that no essential change has occurred in the Moscow Patriarchate since 1924. It must be held, in the light of the evidence, that the Moscow Patriarchate now exists solely by sufferance of the Soviet Government, that it is subject to civil direction and ultimate control by the Soviet.

The House Committee on Un-American Activities in March of 1959 and the U. S. Senate Internal Security Sub-Committee in July of 1959 released the testimony of Petr Deriabin, then the top KGB agent ever to escape from the U.S.S.R. and talk. Deriabin confirmed what the New York Court was to state one year later when he revealed that Secret Police agents were, indeed, running the Russian Orthodox Church and that Metropolitan Nikolai was "a state Security Agent of long standing" with whom Deriabin had to work officially in Vienna during Allied occupation of that city and while Deriabin was in charge of Secret Police activities. Nikolai had come to Vienna to attend one of the usual "Peace" conferences set up by the Soviets and also to deal with another KGB agent serving as a Russian Orthodox priest in Vienna by the name of Father Arseny.

During his testimony before the U. S. Senate committee Deriabin stated flatly:

Most of the priests in the Soviet Union, and the religious
people who help the priests, they are some kind of agents
of KGB or the MGB, or were at that time.

It is impossible in the Soviet Union to serve God without serving the state security.

Deriabin gave a great deal of detail in his testimony concerning the activities of Major General Karpov, KGB official,
who headed the religious section of the Secret Police and
supervised the activities of the Russian Orthodox Church.
Karpov recruited candidates for the ministry who were to
study in the seminaries and serve the KGB at the same time.
These candidates wrote reports to the Council on Orthodox
Affairs headed by General Karpov. Some of these were
willing servants of the KGB, others served under duress.

The New York State Court of Appeals said in the St.
Nicholas Cathedral Case:

> There is an obvious distinction between the civil head of
> an established or State Church sworn to support it, and
> the appointed agent of the State Security system (KGB)
> posing as a cleric to effectuate the policies of the State
> including the ultimate elimination of the very Church
> he subverts.

The very same Major General Karpov of the KGB and
Nikolai, his agent with the religious "front", entertained 11
leaders of the National Council of Churches of the USA at
a state banquet in Moscow in 1956. These same NCC leaders
came back to the United States exulting over the gracious
hospitality of their Soviet hosts and fulminating about "religious freedom" in the Soviet Union.

One of the examples of such hospitality was that mes-
sengers delivered to their Moscow apartment door as gifts
all the things which they had admired the day before in a
Moscow department store. An example cited as proof of

religious freedom in the USSR was the fact that a lay member of the delegation, who was a lawyer, also, saw babies being baptized in Russian Orthodox Churches!

Nikolai was brought to the United States by the National Council of Churches leaders in June of 1956 along with an entourage of lesser lights. Dr. Eugene Carson Blake, who was then president of the National Council of Churches and Stated-Clerk of the United Presbyterian Church, paraded Nikolai through Philadelphia's Independence Square and up the stairs of Independence Hall to the shrine of American freedom, the Liberty Bell. Nikolai, in his impressive long-flowing religious regalia, had his picture taken with his hand on the Liberty Bell, while downstairs several hundred extra Philedelphia policemen held back the crowds of demonstrators, many of whom were escapees from Nikolai's country, carrying signs in Russian and English exposing Nikolai as a Soviet agent dressed in religious robes, and as the one who stood with Khrushchev in the Ukraine during the blood purge of those who would not bow their necks to Moscows yoke. Nikolai had "fingered" the recalcitrant priests!

This was the same Nikolai, Foreign Secretary of the Russian Orthodox Church, who had made vicious tirades against the United States during the Korean campaign!

Two warnings were given publicly to the liberal church leaders in the United States who had been fraternizing with the Moscow religious KGB agents. Both of them were given in the same year, 1959. One was a tremendous exposé of the use of the Russian Orthodox Church by the Soviet State written by Patricia Blake, Moscow correspondent for *LIFE*, and the other was the testimony of Petr Deriabin before the House Committee on Un-American Activities and the U. S. Senate Sub-Committee on Internal Security, which was also carried by *LIFE*.

Miss Blake's article is entitled "Russian Orthodoxy: a Captive Splendor" (*LIFE* September 14, 1959)

The Deriabin article appeared in two successive instalments in *LIFE* for March 23 and 30, 1959 under the caption "Red Agent's Vivid Tale of Terror. A historic defection gives U. S., first full story of secret police."

Miss Blake wrote:

> Orthodoxy's collaboration is insured by a special government ministry and the Communists have utilized the Church ever since as an arm of the Soviet State.
>
> I have seen for myself in Russia, church and state have turned a bloody conflict into a strange and mutually profitable marriage of convenience. . . the church serves as an efficient tool of Soviet policy.
>
> The Commmunists have actually extended the church's power in subjugated areas. In 1946, the 3.6 million Roman Catholics of Galicia (annexed from Poland by the Soviets in 1939) were forced to accept the authority of the Russian Orthodox Church as a means of binding them closer to Moscow. The once independent Eastern Orthodox churches of Albania, Romania and Bulgaria are now dominated by the Russian Church for the same imperialist reasons.

Miss Blake's article points out that the mother church in Moscow was even used to extend the influence of the USSR over those countries which were soon to become satelites by working through the local churches. Scarcely had World War II ended when this extension of Communist power abroad through the churches began.

The spread of this influence was not limited, outside Russia proper, to what were to become the satellite states within a short time. Patricia Blake points out that Moscow's foreign policy was operative in the countries of the Middle East also:

The Kremlin also uses Russian orthodoxy as a sort of cat's paw in all areas that have Orthodox churches. The Russian prelates gladly cooperate in this because for centuries they have chafed at the seniority given the Patriarch of Constantinople by Orthodox groups in general. Patriarch Alexei of Moscow, backed by ample funds, is trying to seize the leadership of Orthodoxy from Constantinople, a move which would be of tremendous service to Soviet ambitions in the Middle East. The Russian church has not only provided lavish junkets around the Soviet Union for Orthodox representatives from all over the Middle East but has also tried to influence church elections there by supporting prelates who would favor Moscow.

The Moscow Patriarchate has embarked upon an ambitious and aggressive program to establish control over all the autonomous churches of the Eastern Orthodox Confession with headquarters in Constantinople. An ancient Russian ambition was to become the inheritor and repository of the Christian tradition and the true center and leader of Christendom. The idea was based upon the notion that both Rome and Constantinople had possessed and then had forfeited the mantle of leadership which thus passed to Russia. The theory embodying the claim was known as "Moscow-the-Third-Rome". There is considerable evidence to show that Patriarch Alexei, serving well the aims and purposes of the expansion policy of the Soviet Union, has become an efficient tool for promulgating it.

The Patriarchate of Moscow has derided the traditional title of the Patriarch of Constantinople as the "Ecumenical Patriarch" and has sought to bring all Orthodox churches under Constantinople (Athenagorus) to Moscow instead. During and after World War II Alexei of Russia sent Foreign Secretary Nikolai to the Middle East for the sole purpose of persuading the Eastern Orthodox churches to leave the jurisdiction of Constantinople and to join Moscow. Nikolai

carried out the same mission in what are now the Eastern
Satellite States in Europe, before they even became that,
through internal subversion master-minded by the Kremlin.

Thus, through visits to these countries outside the
Soviet Union, through cooperation on the part of certain
political figures within these nations, through subsidies
furnished by the Soviet Government, and through infiltration
and pressure, the Moscow Patriarchate is making its influence
felt throughout the Orthodox world, and is now becoming
bold enough to send delegations to the United States because
of the gullibility of the Western World leaders of the National and World Councils of Churches.

Even the attack by the Patriarch of Moscow, Alexei, on
the American Government during the Cuban crisis, did not
wake up Western Church leadership. At the same time that
Alexei sent his famous cable to U Thant, denouncing the
United States, he also sent messages to Dr. W. A. Visser t'
Hooft, general secretary of the World Council of Churches
and to Mr. J. Irwin Miller, president of the National Council
of Churches in the USA, seeking their influence against the
United States.

In the cable to Visser t' Hooft, Metropolitan Nikodim,
successor to the recently deceased Nikolai, expressed 'our
confidence that the World Council of Churches will in the
future not weaken its efforts in the direction of peace as long
as the perilous conflict has not found, with God's help, a
propitious solution'.

Nikodim's message to Irwin Miller said:

We have confidence in the good will of the American
people who are opposed to the possibility of a new war.
It is the duty of American church leaders to use all op-
portunities in pressing the U.S. government to abandon
its crazy policy. We hope the Lord will help you in your
efforts.

The Moscow Patriarchate certainly presumed a lot in telling American church leaders what they should do about American government policy.

The messages were co-signed by the heads of most of the government-recognized religious groups in the Soviet Union such as Zhidkov of the Baptists, Sphriam II of the Georgian Orthodox Church, Vazgen the First of the Armenians, Metropolitan John of the Old Believers, and other puppets from Lithuania, Estonia and Latvia.

Moscow's power through the instrument of a subservient Russian Orthodox Church is now spreading its influence throughout the world under the guises of "Peace", "Cooperation", and "Unity".

"O what a shame!" says Moscow, "that there should be so many divisions in Christendom," and many unlearned and unthinking people in high places in America swallow the bait, get hooked, and are soon found parroting the same phrases.

Upon the occasion of the celebration of the 500th year of autocephaly of the Russian Orthodox Church, Alexei convened a conference in Moscow, attended by most of the representatives of the autocephalous Eastern Orthodox churches. It lasted for ten days from July 8 to July 17, 1948 during which time resolutions were passed on such subjects as the Papacy, the Validity of the Anglican Orders, the Church Calendar, and the Ecumenical Movement. The most virulent attacks were made on the Roman Catholic Church. Overtures were made to the Angelican Hierarchy to establish formally an expression of unity of faith and confession in exchange for Russian Orthodox recognition of the Anglican priesthood.

Final action of the conference was an attack, in the form of a resolution, against the 'Western capitalist and imperialist world' whose children, Catholic and Protestant, 'are instigators of a new war'.

Here is the text of the resolution:

> Whereas the Orthodox East is inspired by the great principles of peace on earth and mutually brotherly love among men, the aggressiveness of the Western capitalist and imperialist world is only too strikingly obvious. It is from these that the danger of a new war with its unheard of terror for long-suffering mankind again approaches.... We ministers of the Orthodox Church are painfully anxious by the fact that the instigators of the new war are children of the Christian world—Catholic and Protestant. We grieve deeply that instead of hearing the voice of peace and Christian love from the fortress Catholicism—the Vatican—and from the nest of Protestantism—America—we hear blessings bestowed on a new war and hymns of praise to atom bombs and similar inventions intended for the extermination of human life. We sincerely pray and most ardently desire that in the love of God and one's neighbor, the pride and ambitions of the Vatican and those who support it may melt; and also that the self-confidence of Protestant rationalism should be replaced by Christian humility, in order that they (both Catholics and Protestants) may say in the words of St. Paul, 'By the grace of God I am what I am.'

Here is the tiresome repetition of the Kremlin phony 'peace' voice, making Moscow the epitome of sweetness and light, while the Western Nations are the big bad boys of war and trouble. We wonder if Alexei and his puppets at this Moscow conference wrote and spoke with tongue in cheek when they quoted from St. Paul, who, obviously, is not here to protest such Communist use of his writings; or if Alexei realized that it was not 'by the Grace of God' that he is what he is and is where he is, but through the permission of Josef Stalin and his successors.

One would think that if Alexei wanted the American section of the Russian Orthodox Church back under his jurisdiction he would think twice before continuing such attacks against the United States. This is no way to win churches and influence worshippers. But, no, such attacks have continued ever since Sergei's regime and have become more and more frequent and virulent under Alexei.

In 1946 fifth column groups seized control of the Ukrainian Church in Galicia. The subverters then appealed to Alexei and Karpov for reunion with Moscow! This group had been cut off from Moscow's jurisdiction ever since the Union of Brest in 1596. Five million Ukranians had no sayso in this plot. They responded by assassinating Archpriest Kostelnik, the chief instigator. Similar procedures were followed in other nations of Eastern Europe such as Czechoslovakia, Poland, Latvia, Lithuania, Rumania, and Estonia.

There are two and one half million Orthodox believers in the United States. Only one small group accepts Moscow's jurisdiction over their church. The vast majority refuse to have anything to do with the Russian Orthodox Church in the USSR until it purges itself of Soviet control.

This does not mean that the Moscow Patriarchate has given up trying to gain control over the Orthodox churches in the United States. By no means. In 1958 a group in New York City loyal to the Moscow hierarchy brought a suit against the American group in control of the Cathedral of St. Nicholas in an attempt to have the courts rule in favor of the Moscow Patriarchate. After 18 months of hearings, the New York State Court of Appeals ruled against the Moscow group and in favor of the local U.S. group in control of the Cathedral. The court stated unequivocally that the Moscow Patriarchate was not free but was rather under the control of the godless Communist state and was carrying out the orders of the Communists.

When the Moscow Patriarchate assigned Archbishop

Boris to take over jurisdiction of the Russian churches in the United States in 1954, the United States Department of State refused to grant him an entrance visa.

A small Rumanian Orthodox group in the United States tried to gain control of church property in the U. S. for the hierarchy in Rumania; that suit also failed. The court stated at the time in its decision:

> The American group had discovered that it was dealing, not with the Holy Synod and Patriarch, but with the Communist government of Roumania, which was dictating the appointment of its bishop in the United States and Canada.

Another device which Moscow has tried to use to soften up church people within the United States in favor of the Soviet regime and its brand of religion has been through the cultural exchange agreement. Long-bearded Soviet priests in flowing vestments have arrived in the United States through the connivings of National and World Councils of Churches people with U. S. Department of State officials.

Testifying before the House of Representatives Sub-Committee on Appropriations in 1963, John Edgar Hoover, Director of the Federal Bureau of Investigation spoke as follows:

> Since 1957, there has been a steady upward trend in the number of Soviet cultural, technical and educational groups visiting the United States. Soviet tourists are also on the increase. The Soviet intelligence services make use of these groups to implement their intelligence operations in this country.

In 1954 when certain notorious Red clergymen, such as Josef Hromadka of Prague, Czechoslovakia, were invited by World Council of Churches representatives in the United States to visit America for the purpose of attending the World Council meeting in Evanston, Illinois, a storm of protest arose in the U. S. Congress, in the nation's press, and in the larger patriotic organizations. The excuse given by the liberals for allowing these Red agents to come to our land was that they might get converted to our "viewpoint" as a result of their visit.

This wishful thinking was exposed as a fraud after the Rev. Dr. Josef Hromadka and the Iron Curtain entourage returned to the irrespective Communist countries and launched in print and orally some of the most vicious attacks against the United States anyone would care to hear or to read. Hromadka called the United States a "nation of gangsters" and even charged that fathers made their little children take medicine at gunpoint! The speeches made by these Red prelates are tragic, but they also read like something out of a comic opera composed in Moscow by the official propaganda bureau of world Communism!

Citizens of the Free World must understand that these Red visitors are hand-picked and are tried and trusted propagandists for the Communist way of life. That is why their families are not permitted to accompany them on these intelligence collecting trips to the United States.

Still, there are some in high ecclesiastical places who will not believe the facts. One such is the former President of the National Council of Churches and presently chief executive officer of the United Presbyterian Church, Dr. E. C. Blake. *The Chicago Tribune* in a lead editorial dated December 1, 1956 stated:

> Leaders of the World and National Councils have long cherished illusions about Communism and the possibility of religious freedom in Communist countries.

The *Tribune* then went on to say that Dr. Blake came back from Moscow in March of 1956 talking nonsense about the position of the churches in Russia. In the light of the Russian onslaught against Hungary the *Tribune* hoped for Dr. Blake's progressive enlightenment.

In July of 1963 Senator Thomas Dodd of Connecticut called upon the U. S. Senate Internal Security Committee to investigate the increasingly frequent visits of delegations of iron curtain clergymen to the United States.

"It can be taken for granted," the Senator declared, "that at least a small quota of our visitors have been communist secret police agents in clerical garb."

The Senator suggested that one purpose of the visits was to extend the influence and control of the "mother churches" in communist bloc countries over the Orthodox church organizations and communities in the United States. Another object was to foster sympathy and support for the governments of the communist countries.

Senator Dodd charged that the Serbian Orthodox Patriarch of Belgrade had suspended the administrators in charge of three Serbian archdioceses on the North American continent and had assumed direct control over them himself. He also added that the Orthodox synod in Bucharest, Roumania had appealed to all Roumanian Orthodox clergymen in this country to accept the authority of the "mother church" in Roumania.

In commenting favorably on the Senator's request for the investigation *The Chicago Tribune* editorialized:

Patriarch Alexis of Moscow at the time of the Korean War accused the United States of germ warfare, called American soldiers savages, denounced Gen. MacArthur as another Hitler, and said the United States, not the North Korean Communists committed aggression.
1956 at the invitation of Dr. Eugene Carson Blake of the Metropolitan Nikolai, who visited the United States in National Council of Churches, was identified as a member of the soviet secret police by Yuri Rastvorov, a former Soviet official who found sanctuary here. Peter Deriabin, a former major general of the soviet police, testified be-

fore the House Committee on Un-American Activities
that he had worked with Nikolai in the secret police
during World War II.

Patriarch Cyril of Bulgaria has served as main speaker
at the soviet propaganda "peace" conferences in Moscow.
At the time of the Cuban crisis last fall, he protested to
the United Nations against the United States blockade.
Many gullible American clerics and other visitors to the
Soviet Union have professed to believe that freedom of
religion is permitted if not encouraged.

It is amazing that one of the largest newspapers in the
world, a secular publication, can see through the religious
front put on by the Soviet agents, warn the public against
their activities; but, many in high religious positions in the
National and World Councils of Churches seem to have no
sense of discernment between the true and the false, the
genuine and the fake when it comes to Iron Curtain clergymen. Hence, they sit down to sup with them, exchange visits,
and parade the Kremlin's religious agents before the American public as bonafied Christians!

It was Christ, the head of the Church, who said: "Ye
shall know them by their fruits." And he explained that a
bad tree cannot bring forth good fruit. The fruits, or evi-
dences of the Soviet Union's religious agents are spread all
over the universal landscape, and much of it has been printed
in their own official journals. Will the religious people in the
Free World wake up to what is going on in time?

Perhaps the greatest indictment of the present heads of
the Russian Orthodox Patriarchate and its supporters in the
Soviet Union and abroad was published in 1952 in Paris by
the YMCA Press. The exact author is not known but it was
published originally by an Orthodox priest within the Soviet
Union whose identity, for obvious reasons, must be protected.

Professor A. V. Kartashev republished it. Here are significant extracts from the manuscript:

> Russia at present needs above all else truth and freedom, and she will secure freedom only by way of truth. As long as we lie, we will be slaves, witnessing to our slavery and strengthening it by our lies. That is why our confessors and martyrs of the last ten years have led us toward freedom, while the hypocrites and liars of our day lead us toward slavery.
>
> Some became martyrs. Others hid in emigration or in the underground—the forests and ravines. The third group went underground—the individual souls who learned the wordless and almost invisible secret prayer, the prayer of hidden fire. At present there has appeared a fourth group: they decided to tell the Bolsheviks, 'Yes, we are with you!' And not only to tell them, but to say and confirm it by deeds; to help them, to serve their objectives, to fulfill all their demands, to lie along with them, to participate in their deceits, to work hand in hand with their political police.
>
> We have seen these people. They all have the typical stone-masked faces and clever eyes. Thy do not restrain themselves, but openly lie, and that about the most serious and sacred—the situation in the Church and the confessors martyred by the Bolsheviks. In their own peculiar way they made their agreement with the Soviet regime, and not troubling themselves about observing the ecclesiastical canons, they 'chose' from among themselves a 'patriarch' acceptable to the Bolsheviks, and officially announced a new, religiously paradoxical and unheard of 'Soviet Church'.
>
> With that consciously false announcement Alexei, and later his emissaries, went abroad. They knew better than anyone else that the Church became a submissive establishment for the Soviet regime: that they were in duty bound and must speak only that lie, and yet they persisted in lying 'about the real freedom of the church.' Such were the performances of Alexei's political emis-

saries in Paris, of those so-called 'metropolitans' and 'bishops'. The same thing occured in America.

And later these 'hierarchs' appeared among us and demanded that we acknowledge their 'authority' and submit to their ecclesiastical leadership in the same way in which they submitted to the Soviet spiritual leadership. But of this latter they kept still.

In answer to such as have forgotten or have become weary, we affirm the thesis: Orthodoxy, which has subjected itself to the Soviets and has become the tool of the world anti-Christian seduction, is not Orthodoxy, but a seductive anti-Christian heresy which decks itself in the torn garments of historic Orthodoxy. If someone really does not see the false role of the new 'patriarch', let him but consider: himself enslaved, WHY does Alexei strive to subjugate to himself and enslave along with himself even the Orthodox Church abroad?

Himself having accepted the compromise with the enemies of Christianity and Orthodoxy, WHY does he force that compromise upon us, who, God be praised, yet have the possibility not to pray for the devil and his successes in the world? Why has it suddenly become necessary to deprive the Orthodox abroad of their freedom of prayerful and ecclesiastical breathing?

These are excellent descriptions of a Church and its false leaders which have become propaganda media for a godless state in order that they might have an outward show of permissive existence. The questions raised by the Orthodox priest will probably never be answered by Alexei, his willing lackeys in the Moscow Patriarchate, the godless leaders of the Kremlin, nor by the blinded liberal clergy of the Western world who think they can do business with the devil's crowd and have good come out of it.

What has been happening to the churches within the Soviet Union while the Moscow Patriarchate has been extending its power and spreading Communist propaganda outside the Iron Curtain?

According to a detailed report compiled by the Institute for the Study of the USSR with headquarters in Munich, Germany and a branch office in New York City, some 2000 churches have been nailed shut in the Soviet Union in the period 1960-1962. The staff of the Institute is made up of former Soviet scholars who publish their findings in various journals in different languages throughout the Free World.

A delegation of the National Council of Churches that visited the Soviet Union was informed by authoritative sources in 1962 that 1,500 churches were closed in the USSR in 1961. Information is received regularly by the Synod of Bishops of the Russian Orthodox Church outside of Russia, located at 75 East 93rd Street in New York City, which tells of continual persecution and harassment of believers in Russia.

The January 23, 1962 issue of *Izvestia*, official Soviet government propaganda organ told how two young Baptist girls stood up against the campaign conducted in the city of Ulovaya (Tula Oblast) against the local Baptist group. Both girls ended up in the hospital and *Izvestia* launched a tirade against the local authorities, accusing them of taking no steps to stop "the blackmailing activities" of the Baptists. *Izvestia* did not interview the so-called Russian Baptist leader, Jacov Zhidkov, on this situation, evidently, as no word of any intercession on his part for these Baptist believers appeared in print.

Zhidkov's record of collaboration with Soviet authorities is a long one, but not quite as lengthy as Nikolai's. They, however, have been close collaborators at various conferences within the Soviet Union and abroad on the "peace" question. Baptist Zhidkov spouts the same "Russia is the leader of peace" and "the United States is the imperialist aggressor" routine which Nikolai, Nikodim, Alexei and Company have been playing over and over again since the end of World

War II. He is the pastor of the only "Baptist" church in Moscow.

No more than 10,000 churches remain open in the Soviet Union according to latest available figures. There were 78,000 in Russia in 1916 when the population was far less than now.

Patricia Blake of *LIFE* described the attitude of a typical young Russian toward what is represented to be the Russian Orthodox Church in the USSR:

> In Kiev (where Christianity first entered Russia in 998 A.D.) a disabused young believer, a professor of Russian literature, told me: "I'll never set foot in an Orthodox church again. How can I feel moved by a service which begins with a blessing for the Presidium of the Communist Party of the U.S.S.R.? How can I confess to a priest who, for all I know, might report me to the secret police?

Practically the entire congregations of those churches which do remain open consist of elderly individuals who pre-date the Bolshevik Revolution. The seeking of converts to the faith among young people is forbidden. Evangelistic work outside the church building is also prohibited. Young people, who, through the influence of their elders, might want to become Christians know the terrible ridicule and persecution they would face, so they leave "religion to the older people," who will soon die off and who need something to solace them in their declining years.

The ironical part about the Soviet State directing the affairs of the churches in the USSR is that the state also urges the forces of atheism to destroy religious belief and to expose it as a superstition, completely unscientific.

How then can the Russian religious leaders serve such a two-headed monster; and, further, how can Western clergymen be taken in by the "freedom of religion in Russia" propaganda?

Chapter V

MOSCOW ENTERS THE WORLD COUNCIL

One of the most important propaganda victories scored by the Communist church leaders was election to membership in the predominantly western World Council of Churches after fifteen years of playing hard to get.

In August of 1948 at Amsterdam, when the World Council was organized, the Russian Church refused to join on the grounds that the council was a "facade for Western Imperialism."

How times have changed! After constant wooing through the years on the part of the liberal clergymen, mostly from the United States, the Russian Orthodox Church and a number of its satellites were received with open arms at New Delhi, India on November 20, 1961, into membership in the World Council with only several abstentions and one lone clergyman carrying a protest sign in front of the meeting hall.

The Russian-controlled Orthodox churches of Latvia,

Lithuania, Armenia and the Province of Georgia, along with what is hypocritically called the All-Union Council of Evangelical Baptists and others have all been received into the WCC since the Russian Church entry. So have the Russian Armenian Orthodox Church, the Polish Orthodox Church, the Bulgarian Orthodox Church, the Roumanian Orthodox Church and the Estonian and Latvian Evangelical Lutheran Churches.

The decision to seek admission to the World Council of Churches was adopted at a Russian Orthodox Synod on March 30, 1961 and ratified by a council of Russian Orthodox Archbishops on July 18, 1961. At the July 18 meeting Patriarch Alexei described the relationship between the Russian Orthodox Church and the ecumenical movement and why the position of the church was changed in regard to membership in the WCC. Here is part of his statement:

> At the present time we have changed our position in relation to the World Council of Churches. However, even previously, we Orthodox Christians had an attitude to Western Christians that was not cold and certainly not scornful. . . . Now, when those who have fallen away from the church are themselves seeking unity with it, we should meet them halfway in order to facilitate their seekings. . . . When the Russian Orthodox Church is admitted to the World Council of Churches, our representatives will witness in it to the truth preserved in the Orthodox Church. . . . Under the present circumstances we cannot help but see indications of the need to encourage a spirit of Christian community and to link the Christians of the East and West. Our mission under present conditions is to show Western Christians the light of Orthodoxy.

This explanation of why the Russian Orthodox Church changed its mind after fifteen years of staying out of the World Council is recorded in the official journal of the

Moscow Patriarchate, Number 8, 1961. It is authentic. It shows that the Russian Church leadership decided that it would be more to the advantage of the Russians to join the WCC. The advantages would include the opportunity to do missionary work within the Council and to show "the light" to those churches of the Western World which the Russian leadership did not believe were in the historic stream of Christianity, but which had fallen away, namely the Protestant churches!

This was a condescending attitude of the Moscow group to take toward Western Protestantism, to say the least! behind this intended theological missionary excuse was the fact that their decision to enter the World Council of Churches reflected a change in state policy. One must never lose sight of the fact that the Russian Orthodox Church is run by and takes its orders from the Soviet authorities, and such a momentous decision to link its activities with churches of the Western World could not be made by Alexsei and his entourage without first consulting Karpov and the political controllers of Church-State relations.

In 1948 at the first General Assembly of the World Council of Churches in Amsterdam the Moscow Patriarchate refused to enter membership and openly declared the WCC "mainly pursues anti-democratic and not ecclesiastical aims," and that the entire ecumenical movement "having lost its ecclesiastical character, has turned into a weapon for creating a single front of Protestant Churches against atheism and Communism." The Patriarchate further charged that the ecumenical movement was too much under the influence of "religious groups interested in solving or formulating political problems agitating public opinion in the West," and that the Patriarchate regarded this as "an encroachment of the vanity of this world upon the sphere of religious relationship."

Here is a definite example of the pot calling the kettle black! Of course, the Moscow Patriarchate could *never* be accused of engaging in "political activity" favorable to the Soviet Union! Perhaps Alexei did not think that anyone outside the Soviet Union would ever read the official proceedings of the Russian Orthodox Church as recorded in its own monthly Journal of the Moscow Patriarchate, filled with anti-Western propaganda and effulgent with political mish-mash on the Communist side! Or, perhaps he did not think that Westerners would be able to read the speeches delivered by himself, Nicolai, Nikodim, Zhidkov and a host of other Red clerics within the Iron Curtain countries and outside, many of them carried by the press agencies of the world in addition to *Pravda, Izvestia* and TASS.

Alexei and his fellow Communist clergymen must have overlooked the fact that the entire proceedings of their "peace" congresses, in which they denounced the United States and England as the world disturbers of the "Peace", were printed by the Moscow Patriarchate, all 287 pages of the Zagorsk one, alone, and in which Stalin, the Soviet Union, and Communism were touted as God's "peace" representative on earth!

Not once did the representatives of the Russian Orthodox Church apologize to the World Council of Churches for the slanders and slurs made against the Council and its member churches time and time again over a period of fifteen years. Even more astounding than that was the grovelling attitude of the liberal Western church leaders who were so glad to get the Russian Orthodox Church into WCC membership that not once did anyone even suggest that an apology was due from the Reds! Not once did WCC leaders question Alexei's reason for joining the WCC: that the Orthodox Church wanted to bring the "truth" to the WCC

churches which they described as "fallen away", or, in
theological language, *apostate*.

Actually, the main purpose for the Soviet Church joining the World Council in 1961 was to find one more propaganda platform from which to spout communist deceit.
The Cincinnati Enquirer warned of this very Russian
Orthodox purpose in a lead editorial, shortly before the
WCC was to convene in New Delhi. Its warnings were soon
to be seen as based on solid fact as judged by Russian actions
in the WCC right after the Orthodox Church was voted in.

The delegation to New Delhi was headed by 33 year-
old Nikodim, successor to Secret Police Agent Nikolai, recently deceased, and new Foreign Secretary for the Church.
Nikodim was an ardent and apt pupil of the wily Nikolai.
There were 16 in the Russian delegation.

Scarcely had the Russian Orthodox Church been voted
into membership when Nikodim arose and addressed the
assembly by reading a message from Patriarch Alexei which
consisted of political statements favorable to the USSR.
Alexei expressed the wish that the WCC Assembly "call
upon the governments of the great powers to convene a
conference on the highest level to solve the problem of
reducing international tension, and begin negotiations at
once on universal and complete disarmament."

Any student of post-World War II history would immediately recognize this statement as containing two of the
propaganda lines of the USSR which its representatives to
the UN and its official organs have repeated over and over
again from Moscow to Geneva to New York to Camp David.

Although the Moscow Patriarchate had time and again
accused churches of the West of using religion to advance the
Imperialistic aims of the capitalist countries, and that the
church should stick strictly to religious activities, the Russian

Orthodox Church did a reverse twist in regard to the World Council of Churches after it got on the inside.

In the Journal of the Moscow Patriarchate, Number 9, for 1961, the Red Church leaders set forth their recommended actions for the WCC as follows:

> It would merit surprise if Christians strove for mutual understanding only in the field of understanding of religious values, paying no attention to the field of international and inter-personal relations. . . . The question of peace throughout the world has been raised with particularly great acuteness just in our time and this, of course, is not a question of politics alone ——The world wars could not but be regarded by Christians as a very great evil. And Christians could not avoid undertaking a struggle against this evil.

This is the same Moscow Patriarchate speaking which so viciously attacked the United States when she intervened in Korea against the invasion of free South Korea by the Moscow-trained and equipped puppet army of North Korea! This is also the same Patriarchate speaking to the WCC which sent the cablegram to U Thant on October 26, 1962, accusing the United States government of committing a "great sin before God" an dof bringing the world to the brink of a nuclear war when President John F. Kennedy ordered Fidel Castro to get his Soviet missiles, which were pointed at the United States, out of Cuba or face invasion.

Of course, according to Moscow intepretation, neither of these acts on the part of the United States could be considered as keeping the "peace". But, when Moscow slaughters the Hungarians or provides Castro or Mao Tse-tung with weapons of war, that is "peace" keeping, according to Alexei and crowd.

The representatives of the Russian Orthodox Church came to the World Council of Churches meeting in New

Delhi claiming to represent two-thirds of the Russian population, although the World Council places the number of Orthodox believers in the USSR at between 30 and 40 million. The higher figure claimed by the Russian delegation was, of course, propaganda for laying claim to bigger representation on the governing body of the World Council, the Central Committee, selection to which is based on total membership in each particular church denomination.

The Soviet delegation met with further success when it influenced the Assembly of the World Council of Churches to adopt a report on foreign policy in which it opposed the arming of West Germany with nuclear weapons, demanded renewal of disarmament talks, and warned against "further acts of provocation" in Berlin.

Alexei's agents also came bearing gifts to the WCC: money, building material and carpets for the World Council's Ecumenical Center Headquarters in Geneva, Switzerland. They were now "in" all the way.

The gullible leaders of the World Council of Churches from the West have said and are still saying that churches function in the USSR and that it is necessary to bridge the gap between the Communist East and the Capitalist West through the churches in both countries; but, what they do not tell the rank and file of church people and religious editors in the West is that the important and ultimate issue is the fact that the churches in Russia are completely dominated by the Soviet Government and that they serve the Communist cause most effectively behind the masquerade of religion. Behind this façade are the activities for subverting the West and the East.

Another significant event at the New Delhi meeting of the World Council of Churches was the election of officers and of members of the powerful governing body, the Central

Committee. The Russians put six representatives on this policy-making group.

Elected president of the World Council for North America was one Charles C. Parlin, a Methodist lawyer and layman who has risen fast in the ecumenical movement ever since he served as counsel for Bishop G. Bromley Oxnam, late president of the WCC, who admitted under oath before the House Committee on Un-American Activities, July 21, 1953, that he had been affiliated with a number of organizations designated as Communist Fronts by Federal Government agencies. Oxnam also admitted that he had served as secretary to Dr. Harry F. Ward who had previously been identified under oath by several government witnesses as not only a member of the Communist Party, USA, but one of the top planning group of the Party while serving as a professor of Christian Social Ethics at Union Theological Seminary in New York City. Oxnam and Parlin were close personal friends for years and Parlin has paid public tribute to him on a number of occasions.

Mr. Parlin has never been cited for any theological knowledge. His picture appeared in the DAILY WORKER, American Communist Party newspaper, for March 8, 1956, showing him with 8 others leaders of the National Council of Churches in the U.S.A. who, upon invitation of Secret Police Agent Nikolai, acting in behalf of Patriarch Alexei, paid a visit to Moscow and the Russian Orthodox Church. Not only was the delegation received by Alexei, but it was also wined and dined by Comrade Major-General Georgi Karpov, overseer for the USSR of the Russian Orthodox Church, and Secret Police member.

This is the same Mr. Parlin who wrote an article for the rabid left-liberal publication known as the *Christian Century*, May 5, 1954 issue, attacking those patriotic and Christian organizations and clergymen who opposed the entrance of Moscow's Red clergy and those of the satellite states into the United States in 1954.

Mr. Parlin was made special chairman of the World Council's Press and Broadcasting Committee in 1954 when the Council met in Evanston, Illinois, and entertained the Red delegates despite thousands of protests registered with the United States Department of State and with the United States Justice Department. Mr. Parlin expressed public indignation over the proposal by U. S. Congressman Alvin Bentley of Michigan, who had served for a number of years in the Diplomatic Corps in certain Iron Curtain countries, and who knew the background of several of the red clerical agents coming to the WCC meeting, that the WCC's Hungarian delegates be invited to appear before the House Committee on Un-American Activities and tell about the so-called "freedom" in Hungary being mouthed by the Red clerical delegates.

WCC President Parlin has steadfastly defended the presence of Iron Curtain clergymen on the governing Central Committee of the World Council of Churches. It is ironical that when the Moscow Patriarchate was attacking the World Council of Churches in 1948 as being a tool of capitalism and the "Imperialistic West", the only good word they had to say was in reference to the presence of Professor Josef Hromadka of the Comenius Theological Seminary in Prague at the Amsterdam organizing meeting of the WCC and his election to the Central Committee. Hromadka's record of service to Red causes pre-dates even Nikolai's and he has never deviated! He has often been identified as the Number One Religious Red propagandist in the satellite countries.

Parlin can sit down with Hromadka and other such red wolves in sheeps:' clothing and work with them as bona fide

Christian clergymen. His criticism has been reserved for the clergymen and Christian laymen who expose the Hromadkas, the Nikolais, the Alexei's and the Oxnams for their perfidy.

It is a strange but significant coincidence that the head of the Russian Orthodox Church, Patriarch Alexei, whose church was received into membership of the WCC at New Delhi, is a lawyer, the same as Charles Parlin! Alexei Sergei Vladamirovich Simansky, received his law degree in 1899 at the University of. Moscow. We wish that a battle of the lawyers would develop within the World Council, one exposing the hypocrisy of the Russian Orthodox Church and its satellites, while the other attempts to defend them, and see which would come out the better legal persuader; one defending the Free World and analyzing the attacks of the Red Clerics on the West, and the other replying to the charges. But, in the light of public utterances and past performances by Mr. Parlin we believe our hopes are in vain.

In January of 1963 Mr. Parlin stood on the stage of the Opera House in Seattle, Washington, and defended another pilgrimage of the Russian clergymen to the United States. They had only brought 8, including Nikolai, in June of 1956. This time, February 1963, they were bringing 16, double the number.

When the delegation arrived in New York it was headed by Archbishop Nikodim, Nikolai's successor. Nikodim was presented with an even greater opportunity than Nikolai had to fool unsuspecting USA clergy and laity with the Communist line and with the false picture of so-called religious freedom in Russia. When Nikolai came in 1956 none of the religious representatives of the Soviet Union and her satellites were members of the World Council of Churches. Nikodim and his entourage were now "in" and "accepted" as bona fide Christian leaders; and, sad to relate, much of the secular press and government people treated them as such.

Several hitches developed in the planned reception of the Soviet clerical agents in a number of U. S. cities, however. The World and National Councils of Churches leaders who had charge of the itinerary tried to keep it secret, but without success. An unnamed individual within the organizations tipped off Dr. Carl McIntire, President of the International Council of Christian Churches, which was formed to oppose the World Council's liberal theological and political views, as to how, when and where the Soviet delegation would arrive. Although it split up into a number of teams, each appearing in several American cities at the same time, Dr. McIntire, in cooperation with refugee groups from the countries which the delegates represented, had a "reception" committee on hand and sizeable demonstrations against the Soviets going in each of the places.

Newspaper coverage of the opposition to the visitors was fairly good in most cities, although some of the press, favorable to the World Council, played down the opposing demonstrations.

Some of the delegates from the USSR were irked at the unfavorable publicity resulting from the opposition, and tried to give the impression through press interviews that the demonstrators did not know what they were doing as all was peace, sweetness and light in the Soviet Union and in the satellite countries. The Soviet delegates were especially annoyed at the presence of clergymen in the ranks of the demonstrators who had escaped with their lives from Lithuania, Latvia, Estonia, Hungary and the USSR after their churches had been taken away from them, confiscated, or puppets installed who would pay obeisance to Moscow.

The most sensational thing of all which developed during the Soviet clerical visit to the United States involved one member of the delegation, a professed Baptist, Arthur Mitzkevitch, and the Reverend Paul Voronaeff, American citizen and minister, whose parents were imprisoned in the Soviet Union. Voronaeff attended a press conference held by the Russian team which was appearing in Austin, Texas. Because of his excellent knowledge of the Russian language he was, on the spur of the moment, invited to translate for the Russians.

The Reverend Voronaeff ingratiated himself with Mitzkevitch to the extent that Mitzkevitch agree to go riding in the evening in Voronaeff's car. When they were alone in the car Mitzkevitch opened up. He identified another member of the delegation, posing as a Baptist, Alexis Stoyan, as a member of the KGB, the Soviet Secret Police.

Mitzkevitch told Voronaeff that he was glad to see the demonstrators against the Soviet delegation and that one of the best things which could happen would be to have more and more such opposition appear in all the cities where the Soviets were scheduled to make stops. He said that no church delegation could leave the Soviet Union and come to the United States or to any other country outside the Iron Curtain unless the delegates were under orders from the leaders of the Soviet Union to propagandize for Communism and against the Free World.

Mitzkevitch told Paul Voronaeff that if he revealed what he had told him then he, Mitzkevitch, would have to deny it publicly for fear of his life and those of his relatives in the USSR.

Voronaeff told his story from the public platforms in Texas, Georgia, Washington, D. C., and New Jersey within a few hours after his revealing conversation with Mitzkevitch. When the press carried Voronaeff's revelations, Mitzkevitch issued a statement denying that he had said such things. He was kept from reporters who tried to interview him and restricted a great deal of the time to his hotel room, under the watchful eye of Stoyan. Mitzkevitch soon disappeared from the public eye and returned to the Soviet Union. Nothing has been heard from him or about him since that time. His name has not appeared in print in any Soviet journals nor in any stories coming out of Russia or from the World Council of Churches.

Confusion exists on the part of leaders of the World and National Councils of Churches, such as Charles Parlin, as to the words "union" and "unity". They say they are striving for Christian "unity" and that we must bring all churches of all nations together in order to have that "unity". A lone verse from Chapter 17 of the Gospel of St. John has been ripped out of its Biblical context and made a mere pretext for organic *union* of religious groups regardless of whether or not they measure up to what a Christian body should be. The commands of Christ, the Head of the church, the warnings and admonitions of the Apostles and writers of Sacred Scripture are all scrapped or shunted aside in an "anything goes" drive for a union of earthly organizations with a religious flavor.

This method of organizing is somewhat like the story of the dog and the cat who were thrown out in the back yard with their tails tied together. Here was a definite case of "union", but certainly not "unity"!

If divisions in the churches have been caused by the departure of some from Christian doctrine, and the turning toward "doctrines of devils", to quote again the Apostle Paul, then such divisions are right and proper. Furthermore, they are based on sound Scriptural grounds.

For example, I John 2:15-19 states clearly:

Love not the world (worldly system) , neither the things that are in the world. If any man love the world, the love of the Father is not in him.

For all that is in the world, the lust of the flesh, and the lust of the eyes, and the pride of life, is not of the Father, but is of the world.

And the world passeth away, and the lust thereof: but he that doeth the will of God abideth forever.

Little children, it is the last time; and as ye have heard that antichrist shall come, even now are there many antichrists, whereby we know that it is the last time.

They went out from us, but they were not of us; for if they had been of us, they would no doubt have continued with us; but they went out, that they might be made manifest that they were not all of us.

Separation of the Sheep, the Scriptural name for the flock of God, from the wolves in sheep's clothing is commanded by the Lord Jesus Christ and his Apostles. He it was who said: "If ye love me, ye will keep my commandments." Love for Christ has been demonstrated down through history by the separation of His people from all sorts of evil and hypocrisy. The fastest growing church movement in the United States is seen in the withdrawal of thousands of people from the old line denominations in the National and World Councils of Churches, and the formation of very large new churches, because of the continual refusal by the old-line denominational leaders to take a stand against cooperation with Communists disguised as religious representatives. This "moving out" procedure is taking place all over the world. The largest Protestant churches in the United States from the standings of actual enrolled membership, buildings and property, missionary and evangelistic endeavors are not in either the National or the World Councils of Churches. The ministers of these churches have taken their

stand against theological and political left-wingism, while
preaching the Gospel of Christ and sound doctrine. These
ministers and churches have become the object of ridicule
by the liberals who are constantly defending Red clerics
and their propaganda line. But, even the secular courts and
government investigative committees have determined that
the stand taken by the separated churches and ministers is
the right one.

Here are the important conclusions of the highest court
in New York State, the Court of Appeals, in the St. Nicholas
Cathedral versus the Moscow group of the Russian Orthodox
Church. The decision is by Chief Justice Conway, Fuld and
Burke concurring. Justice Desmond dissented:

> On the whole record we conclude that the Moscow
> Patriarchate enjoys at best a nominal and conditional
> existence, at the sufferance of the Communist rulers of
> the Soviet State, that the Patriarchate is subject and sub-
> ordinate to the Soviet Government and required to work
> for the furtherance of its political aims and objectives in
> Russia and abroad and that the administration of the
> Church is in the hands of individuals who, through coer-
> cion, through employment or through conviction, sub-
> serve the paramount interests of the State. On this central
> issue, we are contrained to disregard any contrary find-
> ings of the trial justice and as a matter of law act in ac-
> cordance with the facts as clearly and incontrovertibly
> demonstrated.
>
> On the record and exhibits, we think that the domination
> of the Patriarchate by the Communist Government, and
> the necessary subsurvience of the Church in Russia to the
> Soviet State have been conclusively proved and con-
> firmed.
>
> American Courts have a responsibility and duty to pre-
> vent seizure and control by agents of a foreign atheistic
> state acting in the name and guise of a church admini-
> stration they have infiltrated and subverted. What worse

violation of the religious liberties of our people can be envisioned than to require that they subject themselves to the ecclesiastical rule of persons acting for a godless regime as the price of continued use of their churches. No other view is possible than that the Russian Church is administered as an agency of the Soviet State and we are sure that even our dissenting brethren will agree that no court which sits in judgment on this case can be so naive as to disbelieve, any more than did the trial court, by its own statements, the strong proof that the Patriarchate is subsurvient to the Communist dictatorship in the U.S.S.R. If it is conceded, as it thus is, that the Moscow Patriarchate is subsurvient to the Soviet State, and is a tool exploited by the Communist rulers, it is impossible to excuse that condition on the ground that the former Czar of Russia employed the Church as an instrumentality to effectuate the objectives and policies of his government. Common sense tells us that there is an essential and distinguishing difference between the two situations. The Czar did not persecute and harass the Church. On the contrary, he was a member of the Church, a believer of its doctrines, a supporter of its activities and the major source of its revenues. The present Soviet Government is frankly and grossly anti-religious. It attempted to destroy the Church and only tolerates it now because it can be useful.

Everyone in the Western World professing the Christian faith ought to read and re-read the words of the New York Court of Appeals. The evidence was presented in 18 months of hearings. The Court stated that "the facts" were "clearly and incontrovertibly demonstrated". It ruled that the Russian Orthodox Church, as run by the Moscow Patriarchate, is a tool of the godless Soviet State, and that it is administered "by agents of a foreign atheistic state acting in the name and guise of a church administration they have infiltrated and subverted."

This is a strong description of the operations of the Russian Orthodox Church. It is a diametrically opposite conclusion from that of the liberal and leftist leaders of the National and World Councils of Churches who have fawned over the Russian Orthodox leaders and their puppets in the satellite countries.

Such findings of a high court in the United States are not presented by the liberal ministers to members of their congregations who are called upon to put money in the offering plates, portions of which go to subsidize the very Councils of Churches which take the religious Red agents to their bosoms and elect them to their governing bodies.

Unless such evidence, from the courts and from the official publications of the Red churches themselves, is somehow communicated to the masses of Christians in America and what is left of the Free World, then it is possible at some time in the future that our own religious institutions can be subverted from within and become tools for spreading atheistic propaganda; in fact, the trend has already begun as we will soon see from the statements of the Director of the Federal Bureau of Investigation and from the various hearings held under oath before committees of the United States Congress.

Chapter VI

THE SECRET POLICE

A clear picture of the workings of Major General Karpov's supervisory department of Russian Orthodox Church Affairs, and the role of Russian Orthodox priests as informers for the Secret Police, was given in the testimony of Petr Deriabin before the U. S. Senate Sub-Committee on Internal Security on May 5, 1959.

For purposes of identification and to qualify the witness, Deriabin had defected from the Soviet Union while stationed in Vienna, Austria, during Allied Occupation of that city in 1954, where he had been serving as counterintelligence officer for the MVD. Prior to his Vienna duty he had served the MVD in the following capacities:

1. Chief of surveillance group, then chief of administration of Altai Province headquarters.
2. Officer in the counterintelligence section of Okrana in Moscow, the Kremlin Security guard, which took care of the high-ranking members of the Politburo.
3. An officer of the Austro-German section of the intelligence directorate, deputy chief of the German Section.

Deriabin told the Senate Committee:

> In MGB in Moscow, at that time, there was a section
> 0 of the state security. The chief of that section was
> General Karpov, and under him was every security
> officer in the region and the Province sections, or sub-
> sections 0.
>
> This subsection was taking care of all activities of Bap-
> tists and religious orders.

The following dialogue then took place between Deriabin and the Chief Counsel of the Senate Committee, J. G.
Sourwine:

Mr. Sourwine.   What can you tell us about the ramifi-
                  cations of major General Karpov's or-
                  ganization?

Mr. Deriabin.   Well, section 0 was organized April
                  1947. Before that it was another special
                  religious section under the secret police.
                  Before 1947 it was the secret police of
                  the NKVD, we called it at that time. In
                  1947 it was being reorganized. And they
                  started to call it MGB, the Ministry of
                  State Security. And they organized a
                  section—actually started organizing it in
                  1946, and actually completed it some-
                  time in March 1947. And Major Gen-
                  eral Karpov was appointed to be the
                  boss of that section.

                  This section has subsections and other
                  sections. Each republic, for instance,
                  has a section or a subsection. It is ac-
                  cording to the religious activity in each
                  republic. If there is more religious
                  activities in some area, there are more.

And each province has General Karpov's officers in every city where they work in KGB, taking care of all church activities or activists' work.

Most of the priests in the Soviet Union, and the religious people who help the priests, they are some kind of agents of KGB or the MGB, or were at that time.

It is impossible in the Soviet Union to serve God without serving the state security. You give some information for state security about religious activities; otherwise you cannot attend the church. Some of the priests became agents of the state security because there was nothing else for them to do.

When the state security recruited priests and ministers as their agents, they always said, "you will serve us or we will put you in jail, according to your activities."

Mr. Sourwine. In other words, all church activity was subjected and subjugated under an arm of the state?

Mr. Deriabin. That is right.

Mr. Sourwine. And all church activities of the various denominations were coordinated by the state, and they were, also sharply curtailed, were they not—the activities of the churches were cut down—they were prohibited from doing the things they had done before?

Mr. Deriabin.   No; they were never given permission, as you said. It was always, since 1931 or 1932, under state security and the Communist Party.

Mr. Sourwine.   At all times since 1931 or 1932?

Mr. Deriabin.   Yes.

Mr. Sourwine.   Even during the so-called period of tolerance?

Mr. Deriabin.   That was just propaganda.

Mr. Sourwine.   That was just propaganda?

Mr. Deriabin.   That is right. Actually, General Karpov, being boss of the religious sections at the same time, was head of the higher Communist Party school, which is under the central committee of the Soviet Communist Party. It was merely making a gesture about activities and how to make anti-religious propaganda.

Mr. Sourwine.   As I understand it, or understand you to say, no one was allowed to be a priest or to participate substantially in religious activity unless he served the NKVD?

Mr. Deriabin.   I said so. Well, according to my experiences, I met some of these priests and bishops in the Soviet Union, sometimes when they were in Austria, and they were NKVD agents. And I know exactly that all persons who were going into the seminary or attending theological schools, before they go there, they were checked, all of them, and if it is possible, recruit all of them, because it happened like this—all of the people who like to join in the seminary or the theological institute, they write a report to the Council on Orthodox affairs headed by General Karpov, who is on the Council of Ministers. General Karpov is the boss of the section and at the same time he gives orders as to the province sections, to check all the people, and to include them and ask them to serve MGB.

Sometimes, as far as I know, from Karpov's section of security, they started at the theological schools and seminaries, and would spend a few years and become a priest and at the same time they were officers of state security.

Mr. Sourwine. They remained officers of state security while they studied for the priesthood and actually after they became priests?

Mr. Deriabin. That is right.

Mr. Sourwine. I want to be sure I understand this matter of the parallel organizations. You had many local branches of section 0; is that right?

Mr. Deriabin. That is right.

Mr. Sourwine. Then you, also, had General Karpov's Council on Orthodox Affairs?

Mr. Deriabin. That is right.

Mr. Sourwine.   Which paralleled the organization of section 0; is that right?

Mr. Deriabin.   Well, no; it is not exactly right. If you say Soviet Government, this is state security. Here is General Karpov under the Soviet Government, the Council of Ministers. He is boss of the Council on Orthodox Affairs. Here is the top of the section.

Mr. Sourwine.   The same man?

Mr. Deriabin.   The same man.

Mr. Sourwine.   He wears two hats?

Mr. Deriabin.   That is right. Then he has a branch here in all of the provinces to coordinate activities. And he at the same time has branches, you see, how to stop religious activities.

Mr. Sourwine.   Yes.

Mr. Deriabin.   In the same region.

Mr. Sourwine.   On one side as the active head of the church, the state church, he was promoting religion?

Mr. Deriabin.   That is right.

Mr. Sourwine.   And on the other side he was inhibiting religion?

Mr. Deriabin.   That is right.

Much more was told to the Senate Committee by Petr Deriabin whom *LIFE* magazine called the most valuable agent ever to escape from the USSR and talk. For five years he was under maximum security guard in the United States while he was being de-briefed by U. S. intelligence agencies. No one outside of government was permitted to know that he was even in the United States.

How do the collaborators from the liberal clergy in the United States with those Red religious agents of the Soviet Union explain away such testimony? The fact of the matter is, they cannot and do not try. They simply suppress such information and will not even take stock of it when they deliberately pursue the policy of cooperation with Moscow's wolves in sheep's clothing.

This is the very thing our Lord warned about, as did the writers of sacred Scripture. You can't do business with the devil's crowd and expect good to come out of it.

On November 10, 1964, the Senate Sub-Committee on Internal Security released the first of a series of studies on "Church and State in the U.S.S.R." The introduction was written by Senator Thomas Dodd of Connecticut. A few paragraphs from the introduction and the report are apropos at this point:

> In the Soviet Union, all religion and all religious activities are supervised by a "Permanent Committee for Religious Matters" of the Council of Ministers. In every Communist country, the governments have established parallel committees to exercise surveillance over all religious activities.
>
> The Constitution of the Soviet Union theoretically guarantees freedom of religion. But this theoretical guarantee is nullified in practice by a whole series of concrete counter-measures including the wholesale confiscation of church property, and all-pervasive state supervision of residual religious activities, the imprisonment of recalcitrant clergymen.
>
> In addition, the Soviet law specifically prohibits any activities on the part of churchmen or church associations designed to win over "new cadres of working peo-

ple, especially children" to a religious viewpoint. Such propaganda activities, says an official commentary, "shall be considered as a violation of the laws on freedom of conscience and prosecuted in accordance with criminal and civil laws." While "religious propaganda" either inside or outside a church building, is a punishable offense, antireligious propaganda is not only "free" for all citizens but is one of the prime duties of party members and government agencies. It is to be hoped that the present series of studies, heavily documented from many sources, will help to establish the truth about the status of religion under communism and will throw some light on the efforts of clerical authorities in Communist countries to extend their sphere of influence or control over related religious communities in other parts of the world. The Soviet Government has shown a more tolerant attitude toward the Russian Orthodox Church than toward other denominations, especially since the period of World War II when the church declared its full collaboration with the Soviet Government. Although, in general, the Russian Orthodox Church is subject to the same laws and regulations as other churches in the U.S.S.R., some deviations from these general rules are allowed for this church.

The Senate Internal Security Committee is to be congratulated for making such documented and authoritative studies available; but, unless the church people within the United States are told by their clerical leaders that such studies are available and should be studied by every thinking church member who loves freedom and liberty, then such valuable information will gather dust in the storage rooms of committees and the Government Printing Office in Washington D. C. The problem facing the Western World today is not one of lack of information on what the communists are doing and the many devices they use, such as churches, to accomplish their ends. The problem is the means of communicating such information to the rank and file of people. A country can perish for lack of knowledge, and knowledge we must have if the United States and its allies are to survive the on-slaughts of the Communist world conspiracy.

It is interesting to note that Petr Deriabin described in detail how the MVD used Russian Orthodox priests and seminarians to do their dirty work. We should be reminded of the fact that the late Josef Stalin was once a seminarian in a Russian Orthodox Theological school, also, and that ac-cording to the testimony given by Joseph Zack Kornfeder on July 6, 1953 to the House of Representatives Committee on Un-American Activities, Stalin was in charge of the Living Church Movement in the Politburo. In other words, Stalin was the predecessor of Major-General Georgi Karpov, and this was the first important job Stalin held in the Politburo on his climb up the ladder to the Dictatorship of the Soviet Union! Imagine, Stalin, who ordered Russian citizens exe-cuted by the thousands, including his first wife, being a *church* leader!

No doubt if some of the Western leftist clergymen who are now fraternizing with Alexei and his crowd had been able to make contact with Joe Stalin while he was in charge of the Living Church Movement, they would have invited him on a speaking tour of the United States and perhaps even have bestowed an honorary theological degree upon him! Stranger things than this are now happening between clergymen of this stripe in the United States and Britain, and those within the Soviet Union.

The New York City Hearings conducted by the House Committee on Un-American Activities in July of 1953 revealed that some American seminary professors were actual-ly going to the Kremlin on pilgrimages, receiving their orders direct from Stalin, and then travelling as far as China to scatter communist seeds in that great country which was to reap the harvest several decades later of the crop sown by American Soviet sympathizers earlier.

Chapter VII

THE SOVIET "PEACE" GIMMICK

"For from the least of them even unto the greatest of them every one is given to covetousness; and from the prophet even unto the priest every one dealeth falsely. They have healed also the hurt of the daughter of my people slightly, saying, Peace, peace; when there is no peace. They say still unto them that despise me, The Lord hath said, Ye shall have peace; I have not sent these prophets, yet they ran; I have not spoken to them, yet they prophesied,"——Jeremiah 6:13, 14; 23:17, 21

A peaceful world has been the dream of millions of war-wearied people down through the ages of time. Who should be opposed to peace?

But, words are often stolen out of their Biblical and dictionary settings and meanings by scoundrels who are plotting to overthrow or to take over a "peaceful" nation which is unaware that the "peace" overtures of the eventual enemy are but part of a military strategy to disarm the intended victim.

In the days of Israel, the prophets of the Lord were continually warning the populace against the false prophets in their midst who were using the "peace" theme to keep the facts of impending judgment from the people. Jeremiah would never have won friends and influenced people if he were alive today. His was a most unpopular message. He stood in the great market place of Jerusalem and warned that unless the people turned back to the one and only true God and his precepts, that a foreign power by the name of Babylonia would invade their country, lay waste to the land, burn their cities, with not one stone to be left upon another and take the people away captive.

The "peacenik" prophets, described in the above text, ridiculed God's true prophet publicly; and sadly, the people believed the false prophets until the day the enemy came in and carried out to the letter the warnings of Jeremiah.

We might well pose the question at this point: Is history repeating itself? Is the Western World following the same siren song of the false prophets of a false peace to destruction and captivity?

Some squeamish souls who want to avoid what they call "controversy" or criticism of "religious" leaders, are perfectly willing to follow blindly the Pied Pipers of a false "peace", because they are adorned in religious raiment. The Soviet strategists, who are well aware of this attitude, are exploiting the "peace" theme today as never before.

There have been many conferences for "peace" held within the Soviet Union and in the satellite states by communist propagandists dressed in religious garb since the end of World War II. Time and space would never permit a complete discussion of the proceedings of all of these conferences nor a summary of the resolutions passed. Suffice it to say that the theme has been, without deviation, that the USSR

represents the true exponent and example of "peace" in
the world while the nations outside the Iron Curtain, led
by the United States and Great Britain, represent the warmongers who are plotting right now to blow up the world
because of their "imperialist" designs.

Such was the theme in speech after speech made at the
"Conference In Defence Of Peace Of All Churches and
Religious Associations in the USSR" which was held in
Troitse-Sergiyeva Monastery in Zagorsk, May 9-12, 1952.
Those who attended were the leaders of all recognized relig-
ions in the Soviet Union. They are unanimous in their
condemnation of the United States and their praise of the
Soviets; yet a great many of them have been welcomed into
membership in the World Council of Churches.

As if the orations by the Soviet religious puppets were
not enough, as presented from the platform to the ecclesiastical gathering, the Moscow Patriarchate had the audacity to
publish a volume based on the stenographic records of the
Conference proceedings, so that there could be no doubt as to
what was said about the Western World! Furthermore, the
proceedings were translated into many languages, including
English. A total of 43 speeches were made on the subject of
"peace" within the four-day period.

The conference was called by Alexei. Invitations were
accepted by the following delegations of Churches and
religious associations of the Soviet Union:

The Russian Orthodox Church: Alexei, Patriarch of Moscow and all Russia.

> Nikolai, Metropolitan of Krutitzy and Kolomna, mem-
> ber of the World Peace Council, and Chairman of the
> Organizing and Arrangements Committee.
> Gregory, Metropolitan of Leningrad and Novgorod
> Bartholomew, Metropolitan of Novosibirsk and Barnaul
> Pitirim, Archbishop of Minsk and Byelorussia

Filaret, Archbishop of Riga and Latvia

Flavian, Bishop of Oryol and Bryansk

Michael, Bishop of Sambor and Drogobych

Protopresbyter Nicholas Kolchitsky, Provost of the Moscow Patriarchate

Archpriest Constantine Ruzhitsky, Rector of the Theological Academy and Seminary in Moscow

The Georgian Orthodox Church

His Holiness, Melkhisedek (Pkhaladze), Catholicos-Patriarch of All Georgia

Gabriel, Bishop of Alaverdi

Archimandrite Zenobius

Archpriest Nicholas Magaldadze

Archpriest John Sakvarelidze

The Armenian Church

His Holiness, George VI (Cheorekchyan), Supreme Patriarch-Catholicos of All Armenians

Archbishop Konstanyan (Garnik), member of the Supreme Council of the Armenian Church

Bishop Ter-Avanesyan, member of the Echmiadzin Congregation

Head Archimandrite Ter-Saakyan Vardan, member of the Echmiadzin Congregation and Father-Superior of the Monastery-Cathedral of St. George in Tbilisi

Professor Ashot Gareginovich Abraamyan, Assistant Executive Editor of the journal *Echmiadzin*

The Evangelical Lutheran Church in Latvia

Gustavs Turs, Archbishop of the Evangelical Lutheran Church in Latvia and President of Her Supreme Council

Alfons Vecmanis, Church Superintendent of Kandava District and member of the Supreme Church Council

Arvids Kaulins, Church Superintendent of Riga and member of the Supreme Church Council

The Evangelical Lutheran Church in Estonia

Jaan Kiivit, Archbishop of the Estonian Evangelical Lutheran Church

Pastor George Klaus, Superintendent, and associate member of the Presidium of the Consistory of the Evangelical Lutheran Church in Estonia

Pastor Julius Voolaid, associate member of the Consistory of the Evangelical Lutheran Church in Estonia

The Catholic Church in Latvia

Bishop Peteris Strods, Deputy of the Metropolitan of Riga and Vicar-Apostolic of the Liepaja Diocese

Julians Vaivods, Vicar-General of the Bishop of the Liepaja Diocese, Chancellor of the Curia, and Dean of the Cathedral Church

The Catholic Church in Lithuania

(The Vilnius Archdiocese and the Panevezys Diocese)

Capitulary Vicar Kazimieras Juozapo Paltarokas, Bishop-Ordinary of the Panevezys Diocese and Administrator of the Vilnius Archdiocese

Jan Ellert, Canon of the Vilnius Chapter and Dean of the Church of the Holy Ghost in Vilnius

(The Kaunas Archdiocese and the Dioceses of Kaisedorys and Vilkavisiskis)

Canon Juozas Jono Stankevicius, Administrator of the Kaunas Archdiocese and of the Kaisedorys and Vilkavisisk is Dioceses of Lithuania

(The Telshei Diocese)

Canon Petras Mazelis, Administrator of the Telshei Diocese

The All-Union Council of Evangelical Christian Baptists

Jacob Zhidkov, Chairman of the All-Union Council of Evangelical Christian Baptists

Alexander Karev, Secretary-General of the All-Union Council of Evangelical Christian Baptists

Alexei Andreyev, member of the All-Union Council of Evangelical Christian Baptists of Kiev

Nikolai Levindanto, member of the All-Union Council of Christian Baptists of Riga

Senior Presbyter Victor Chechnev, member of the All-Union Council of Evangelical Christian Baptists of Minsk

The Old-Believer Church of Belokrinitsa Concord
(The Old-Believer Archbishopric of Moscow and All Russia)

Flavian (Slesaryev), the Old-Believer Archbishop of Moscow and All Russia

Joseph (Morzhanov), Bishop of Kishinev, Odessa and Chernovitsi, Bishop pro tempore of Ismail, and Assistant to the Old-Believer Archbishop of Moscow and All Russia

Archpriest Basil Korolyov, Dean of the Pokrov Cathedral Church at Rogozhskoye Cemetery in Moscow

The Old-Believer Church of Ancient Orthodox Christians

John, Archbishop of Moscow and All Russia

Leontius Dorofeyev, Dean of the Moscow Temple

The Moscow Preobrazhenskoye Community of Old Believers of the Staropomorsk Concord

Maxim Sergeyev, President of the Executive Board

Ivan Nikolayev, Vice-Chairman of the Congregation of the Church of Exaltation of the Cross

The Grebenshchikov Community of Old Believers in Riga

Ivan Vakonya, Senior Spiritual Leader and President of the Community Council

Porfiry Fadeyev, Spiritual Leader of the Community

The Old-Believer Church in Lithuania

Feodor Kuznetsov, Spiritual Leader and President of the Supreme Council of Old Believers in Lithuania

Ivan Yegorov, Provost of the Council of Old Believers in Lithuania

The All-Union Council of the Seventh-Day Adventists

Paul Matsanov, Ordained Presbyter and President of the All-Union Council of the Seventh-Day Adventists

Vasili Yakovenko, Deputy of the All-Union Council of the Seventh-Day Adventists

The Reformed (Calvinist) Church of the Transcarpathian Region

Adalbert Ghenchi, Dean of the Reformed Church of Transcarpathia

Nicholas Shtefan, Priest of the Church

The Methodist Church in Estonia

Superintendènt Kulgre

Pastor Ferdinand Tombo

The Community of Spiritual-Christians (Molokans) of Tbilisi

Ivan Manayenki, President of the Community's Executive Board

The Community of Spirit-Christians (Molokans) of Tbilisi

Alexei Remizov, President of the Community's Executive Board

The Moslem Council for The European Part of the U.S.S.R. and Siberia

Shakiribn Shaikhlislam Khiyaletdinov, Muft al Hafiz Kala Mullah, and President of the Council

Yarulla ibn Suleiman Yusupov, the Cazi-Muztahid of Penza, Saratov, Tambov and Ulyanov Regions, and High Priest of the Grand Truyev Mosque

Marjan Kiyam ibn Abdul Kadyr Kadyrov, the Cazi-Mujtahid of the Tatar and Udmurt Autonomous Republics and Molotov Region, and High Priest of the Kazan Mosque

The Moslem Council for Central Asia and Kazakhstan

Babakhamov Ziyavitdin, Mujtahid Hafiz and Vice President of the Moslem Council for Central Asia and Kazakhstan

Maksud Nazarbekov, Imam-khatib and member of the Moslem Council for Central Asia and Kazakhstan, and its Representative in Kirghiz Republic

Saken Sagdivakkas Gilmanov, Imam-khatib, member of the Moslem Council for Central Asia and Kazakhstan and its Representative in the Kazakh Republic

Abdurashid Musabekov, Cazi and member of the Moslem Council for Central Asia and Kazakhstan, and its Representative in the Tajik Republic

Abdurakhman Sharipov, Immam and Deputy Representative of the Moslem Council in the Turkman Republic

The Moslem Council for North Caucasus and Daghestan

Mohamed-Gadji Kurbanov, Mufti and Acting President of the Moslem Council for North Caucasus and Daghestan

Shamsutdin Abdullayev, Secretary of the Moslem Council for North Caucasus and Daghestan

Effendi Adam Tlymakhovich Khachukov, High Priest of the Mosque in Psyzh, Cherkess Autonomous Region, Staropol Territory

The Moslem Council for Transcaucasia

Ali Zade Akhund Aga Djavad ogly, Sheikh ul Islam and President of the Moslem Council for Transcaucasia

Effendi Zade Ibragim Abdul Kerim ogly, Mufti, and Vice-President of the Moslem Council for Transcaucasia

Ali-Alekser Abas Magarammov ogly, Cazi and member of the Moslem Council for Transcaucasia

The Central Buddhist Council of the U.S.S.R.

Gabzhi Darmayev Lobsan-Nima, Bandido-Hambo Lama, and President of the Central Buddhist Council of the U.S.S.R.

Gabit Zhigzhitov Sambu, Did-Hambo Lama of Chita Region, and High Priest of the Aga Temple

The Jewish Community of Moscow

> Solomon Shliffer, Rabbi of the Moscow Choral Synagogue and President of the Jewish Community of Moscow

The Jewish Community of Kiev

> Itsko Shekhtman, Rabbi of the Kiev Synagogue

One must readily admit, after having looked over the august list of titles and positions represented by the conferees that here was, indeed, an impressive array of Soviet religious leaders which included just about every brand of religion in the USSR and in some of its satellites. If one, however, were to take the time to give a case history of collaboration with the Communist State on the part of each delegate attending, it would take a veritable encyclopedia to cover the details. Such familiar names as Nikolai, Alexei, Zhidkov, Gustav Turs and Alexander Karev were in the forefront on the program, but many less known titled clerics joined the lusty chorus against the West, day after day.

Soviet Secret Police Agent Metropolitan Nikolai opened the first day's proceedings with a special welcome to the "esteemed guests from foreign lands" who were invited to "unite with us in the great cause of defending peace the world over."

This statement brought the crowd to its feet in applause and the choir immediately chimed in with the National Anthem of the Soviet Union, a fitting beginning for a strategy-for-peace-conference, a la Russe! Naturally, the choir could not be expected to sing the Doxology or the Gloria as that would constitute "religious" propaganda!

The next major item on the agenda was the unanimous election of the single slate of handpicked committee members.

Then Alexei arose and gave a short speech on why it was necessary to call such a "peace" conference, the reason: The enemies of "peace", the Western nations, were at work in trying to bring about a "devastating war". Differences in religion, he said, did not matter when it came to strengthening "peace", therefore they were welcoming the Buddhists and the Moslems. This is significant in that the Soviet and Chinese Communists were to use Buddhist priests in South Vietnam some years later to bring about the overthrow of the anti-communist Diem government of that country. Gullible American newspaper correspondents in Vietnam swallowed wholesale the propaganda that the Buddhists were being persecuted for their religious views by the Diem regime, while, in actuality, the saffron-garbed demonstrators were agents of the Communist conspiracy.

Alexei came up with the notorious lie against the United States armed forces in Korea, that has oft been repeated by the communist propagandists around the globe: that the U. S. was using bacteriological warfare in Korea.

Here are his words:

The unjust war in Korea, the employment of the bacteriological weapon in Korea as well as in China, the preparations for another world war—these are the facts which cannot be qualified otherwise than crimes against love and truth, and there can be no doubt that the struggle against these crimes must be the obligatory and sacred duty of every religious person precisely because of his faith.

Alexei's so-called "facts" were obtained right from the mouth of the Kremlin Communist leaders and not from an on-the-site inspection in Korea. To accept the lies of the Kremlin and then attempt to persuade the religious leaders of the Soviet bloc that it was their "sacred duty" to struggle "against these (alleged) crimes" shows the sheerest hypocrisy and deviltry on the part of the head of the Russian Orthodox Church. Yet, liberal Western clerics of the National and World Councils of Churches can walk arm and arm with such hypocrites and slander anyone who calls their perfidy to the attention of church people.

Alexsei's short diatribe was only the beginning of what gathered momentum. It merely set the Kremlin-planned theme. The highlight was the marathon presentation of Secret Police Agent Nikolai, which consumed 57 pages of the official proceedings. The slanders and abuse heaped upon the United States, Great Britain, and the other Western allies, was scandalous to the ultimate degree. The Foreign Secretary of the Russian Orthodox Church spared no vicious epithet against America in his charges hurled from the platform of this so-called "peace" conference. Nothing could possibly have been more "war-like", unless it had been the ravings of an Adolph Hitler, a Fidel Castro, or a Nikita Khrushchev.

Here are some of the charges made by Nikolai:

1. A third world war was being hatched against the Soviet Union by the Western nations as World War II ended.

2. The United Nations, supposedly set up for maintaining world peace became "the obedient tool for the advocates of a new war."

3. "The cold war was launched against the Soviet Union and the People's Democracies" by those who wanted "to control the destiny of the peoples."

4. The method was adopted "of scaring the peoples with the latest weapons of mass extermination."
   [Of course, the USSR, you understand, was not doing anything like that while she was supplying the North Korean forces with the arms and equipment to attack South Korea, or while her spies in the United States,

> *the Rosenbergs, and the Klaus Fuchs of Great Britain were turning over to her the Western Allies' atom bomb secrets!*]

5. The world was split up into two camps: "the war camp and the peace camp."

6. "We (*the Soviet Religious puppets*) stand outside of politics."
(*The most ridiculous statement of the conference.*)

7. "One side is on principle opposed to war. . . . The other side, however, is obviously afraid of peace."

8. The war side is doing all in its power to bring about another war; it is forging new weapons for the destruction of life and property; "it is employing the most terrible and inhuman means of killing people, condemned by morality and religion."

9. The reason why the "war side" (*the United States and the Western Allies*) is so afraid of "peace" is that it has "a deliberate design to subjugate and dictate its way of life to all the peoples, to the whole world. The reason is thirst for world domination."

10. This war philosophy of the West "is a direct negation of the Gospel, a direct negation of the power of love, which is the basis of the Christian religion."

11. "The deliberate striving for war" on the part of the Western Powers "is due to the fact that they are doomed. It is the consciousness that they are doomed that tempts these people to make war their last card in their gamble for world domination."

12. The Soviet clergymen must reach the people in these doomed countries so that they can "compel their governments" to abandon their war-like policies.

After verbally slaughtering the United States and Britain, Nikolai then devoted 45 minutes to the subject: "The Achievements of the Peoples, Headed by the USSR, In Defending Peace."

Here are some of the highlights of this phase of his harangue:

> In contrast to the imperialist policy of war, the Soviet State, from the very first days of its existence, has striven for peace, for friendship and cooperation among nations. Later, at all stages of its development, the Soviet State continued to pursue a consistent peace policy, being guided by the doctrine taught by V. I. Lenin and J. V. Stalin...this policy found expression in the repeated proposals the Soviet Union has made in the United Nations for reduction of armaments, for the banning of the atomic weapon, and other proposals for strengthening world peace.

> The imperialist countries, however, repudiating all the agreements concluded with the Soviet Union, are obstinately continuing their armaments drive with the object of unleashing a new world war.

At this stage it gets a little hard to take, but we must continue to endure Nikolai's statements, perhaps best by substituting the name of the Soviet Union in the charges, for they describe the actions of the USSR since World War II to a T. Nikolai seems to have his "sides" mixed up!

He continues:

> The peace policy pursued by the Soviet Union inspires and strengthens the hope that it will truimph.
> The Wroclaw Congress of Cultural Workers of April 1948, the Women's Congress in Budapest, held in December 1948, the First World Peace Congress, held in Paris and Prague in April 1949, the setting up of the Permanent Committee of the World Peace Congress" were all inspired by the Soviet Union.

> The Soviet Union, that great power in which there are not, nor can there be, any supporters of aggressive war. The peoples in many countries, indebted to the Soviet Union for their liberation from fascist tyranny and looking upon it as the bulwark of international peace and the

standard-bearer of peaceful constructive labour, followed its lead in the stubborn fight for world peace.

*[At this point someone should have reminded Nikolai
that the United States was in World War II also, and
that American lend-lease to Russia was not manufactured
in Moscow or in Bucharest!]*

The common people in all the countries of our continent
begin to join these people *(the "common people" defined in realistic terms as "the communists within those
captive countries")*. In all parts of the globe, the name
of J. V. Stalin became the banner of the fight for peace.
(Applause)

*Why the applause? Was it a comic opera which was being
staged with Nikolai as the jester? Khrushchev was not in
agreement with this assessment of Stalin when he de-
Stalinized him. It appears that Nikolai was the top build-
er of the "cult of personality" which Mr. K. was later to
deplore.*

Nikolai then went on to recount "the situation created
by the warmongers" through such acts as the ratification of
the Atlantic Pact; the restoration of the military might of
the Japanese "and the West German butchers of mankind";
"the war against the Greek people" (meaning U. S. help to
the Greek nation in its war against the Communists); the
imperialist colonial policy which continued "to fan the
flames of war in Vietnam, Greece, Indonesia and Malaya";
and "the armaments drive doomed the people to still greater
exploitation and poverty."

Of course, Nikolai was careful not to mention that the
Soviet Union was supplying armaments and even advisors to
those groups engaged in internal subversion within the countries he named, and that the Soviet Union had its own
gigantic "armaments drive" on at the expense of the civilian
economy. Oftentimes, the sins of omission are greater than
the sins of commission. Nikolai, on this occasion, was extremely guilty of both.

His speech contained high praise for the Chinese Communists whom he referred to as the Chinese People's Republic, stating further that it joined "the common Peace front that is headed by the Soviet Union." Unfortunately, Nikolai isn't around anymore to explain what happened to that "common peace front" between the Soviet Union and the Red Chinese in recent years.

According to Nikolai, the formation of the Communist regime in East Germany added more people to the "peace front" in October, 1949. Here are his descriptive words of that event:

> In the very heart of Europe arose a peace-loving state, the existence of which, together with the existence of the peace-loving Soviet Union, inspired the peoples of Europe with the hope that the efforts which hitherto had been devoted to war and destruction could now be turned to peaceful construction.

So "peace-loving" was Communist East Germany that the Communists had to build a wall around it to keep the "peace lovers" from getting out! Some of them made it across to the horrible Western Side, although the "peaceful Communists" used "peaceful" machine guns to mow them down when they wouldn't accept the kind of "peace" the Communists had forced upon the citizens of East Germany.

Nikolai spent a great deal of the time recounting the "peace" outfits which Moscow had going from Peking to Paris, from Stockholm to London, from Prague to Paris, and from Warsaw to New York. He gave as outstanding examples of the proponents of peace: the Red Dean of Canterbury, Dr. Hewlett Johnson; and the Federal Council of Churches of the U.S.A.! Imagine the Federal Council of Churches, the predecessor of the National Council, having as one of its rooters, Soviet Secret Police Agent Nikolai! Nikolai was careful to drop some statistics in relation to the Federal Council of Churches when he said they unite "about 30,000,000 Protestants". Perhaps he had borrowed this propaganda trick from the Federal Council's publicity propagandists who frequently were quoted in the American press and represented themselves before U. S. Government agencies as speaking for that many church people, who, incidentally, had never been consulted on any of the positions taken by their self-appointed spokesmen.

In regard to the Red Dean of Canterbury, an openly admitted Communist spokesman, Nikolai confirmed the charges long before made by U. S. Government security groups and by conservative clergymen:

> Tireless activities in this direction were conducted by Dr. Hewlett Johnson, Dean of Canterbury. By his innumerable speeches in defence of peace and of the interests of the common people of all nations, he acquired great influence over the minds of the people in Great Britain, Western Europe and America.

Anti-Communist witnesses before U. S. Government investigating committees, including former American Communist Party leaders who left the Party in disgust, had given sworn testimony over and over again that the Red Dean did have considerable "influence" for the cause of Communism in various countries of the world. Liberal leftist preachers denied the charge and even formed welcoming committees in the United States when Hewlett Johnson paid a visit and spouted his communist line. What better confirmation of the Red Dean's activities in behalf of the Communists could we have than from Secret Police Agent Metropolitan Nikolai, who would certainly know about such activities, if anybody should!

As for the Federal Council of Churches, there are reams

of evidence available on its personnel and activities in behalf of the Communist cause, all the way from the Office of Naval Intelligence to the official resolutions and publications of the Council. In fact, documentary books have been written on the Federal Council of Churches' pro-red activities. Nikolai was certainly in a position to know who was friendly to the Soviet "peace-lovers"!

Nikolai claimed that 500,000,000 people throughout the world signed the Soviet-originated and directed Stockholm Peace Appeal. Now, just how Nikolai and his cohorts of the Kremlin arrived at that total, we probably will never know. It only raises the question: Does the Kremlin have all of these names alphabetized, catalogued on file cards, and filed in the intelligence section of the Soviet Propaganda Bureau?

We do know, and have the evidence, that hundreds of left-liberal clergymen within the United States affixed their signatures to the Red "peace" petition sheets, and those sheets are on file in Government security agencies. They are listed state by state, city by city, and denomination by denomination. Some of the signatories have howled to high heaven when their names were read off the petitions to the people in their own home towns, and when members of their own congregations asked them: "How come?"

Nikolai gave page after page of examples of church groups within the United States and Europe which dutifully followed the Kremlin line on "peace", and which used the prestige of their communicants, who never knew to what they were being committed, to pressure their own governments into accepting the Kremlin's suggestions. Nikolai named a congress of delegates from 17 Protestant groups in the United States, special meetings of Presbyterian and American Methodist groups which made demands upon the American Government in line with Moscow's proposals on disarmament, banning the bomb, etc.

As for European church leaders he singled out for special praise Martin Niemoller and Bishop Otto Dibelius of Germany, and Hugo van Dalen of the Reformed Church of Holland who just happened to be in the audience at Zagorsk when Nikolai made his marathon address.

Quaker groups in England were not omitted in the honor roll, as called by Nikolai. He especially praised the English group which paid a visit to the Soviet Union, as the American Friends Service Committee has done, and returned home to say nice things about the Soviets.

Rabbis of France and Poland were quoted by Nikolai as saying that the Stockholm "demand, meets the age-long aspirations of the Israelite people."

The Mohammedans in the USSR, Middle East and North Africa came in for their share of praise for "peace efforts", as did the Buddhists of Mongolia, Ceylon, and Burma.

The last hour of Nikolai's diatribe was in praise of the Russian Orthodox Church within the Soviet Union for promoting "peace". Nikolai praised himself for being the chief leader for "peace" within the Church. At the first U.S.S.R. Conference for Peace, Nikolai headed the delegation and made the major address, as usual, in which he called upon "the many thousands of honest Catholic and Protestant clergymen, and the vast millions of their flocks, to fight the temptation to commit the crime of Cain and engage in fratricide, and to exert all efforts to strengthen the sacred cause of peace." What that had to do with "peace" *within* the Soviet Union was not explained by the Metropolitan.

Nikolai repeated the Big Lies against the United States:

In connection with the bloody events in Korea, the Patriarch and the Holy Synod of the Russian Orthodox Church wrote to the Security Council of the United Nations expressing sympathy with the martyred Korean people, protesting against American aggression in Korea, and, in the name of Christ, demanding the cessation of this unlawful war.

At the Second USSR Conference for Peace it was my duty, as representative of the Russian Orthodox Church, to explain Her principles and practice in relation to the criminal fomenters of a new war, in relation to the aims of the struggle for peace and to American aggression in Korea.

This has been a favorite sport of the leaders of the Russian Orthodox Church in recent years: to send messages to the United Nations accusing the American people of something they did not start, or do. We have already seen this in regard to the hypocritical communication sent by Alexei, Vasgen I, and Jacov Zhidkov to U Thant when President John F. Kennedy ordered Castro to get his guided missiles pointed at the United States out of Cuba, or else!

In every case, since World War II, in which the United States has come to the aid of peoples being attacked or subverted by Communist aggression the Russian Orthodox Church leaders have issued statements labeling the American Nation as the aggressor.

Here is the florid language of Nikolai in another attack upon the United States in his seemingly endless harangue at the Zagorsk "Peace" conference:

When the American cannibals resorted to bacteriological war against the Korean and Chinese people, our Church issued an angry protest, which was published in the press on March 21, 1952.

And so, step by step, the Russian Orthodox Church accompanies her people in the defence of peace, helping to strengthen peace by her moral authority and the unanimity of Her followers.

There is nothing *moral* or *Christian* about the satanic lies against the United States told by the Russian Orthodox Church leaders. The United States did not resort to any type of bacteriological warfare in Korea, or against the Chinese people. This is a complete fabrication dreamed up by the Kremlin criminals. Another such fantasy perpetuated by the Patriarchate of Moscow was that the American Government wanted to solve the population explosion in the world by dropping atom bombs and killing off the excess people. Not once, but many times did Nikolai and Alexei make this charge publicly in the various "peace" conferences set up by them.

Other unbelievable charges made against the United States included the following:

1. "While claiming to be leaders of the blind, a light for those in darkness, teachers of the ignorant, and tutors to the young, are selling poisoned food, are preparing to drop atomic bombs upon the world, are killing babes, women and the aged in Korea, and are destroying all life, even plant life."
2. "Enemies of culture."
3. "Servants of the Devil."
4. "Warmongers."
5. "Trying to hurl mankind into another holacaust."
6. "The American aggressors began to employ germ weapons in Korea . . . this heinous crime."
7. "A crime against Christian morality."
8. "The sons of Turkish Moslems are being sent to Korea to kill peaceful people in the interests of the American capitalists."
9. "Have invented a cheap means of exterminating human beings, while leaving their material property untouched. These designs are prompted by such hatred of mankind, by such malice, as has not been witnessed since the world was created!"

Nikolai concluded Part III of his "Peace" speech by urging the churches and their leaders to go all out in the political field. The faithful must be instructed in international affairs, under the guise of furthering peace. Demands, protests, and the "exerting of all strength" are some of the measures to be used. The agenda will be formulated in the Kremlin and the religious agents will give the cues to the flocks as to when to demonstrate and holler!

First prize statement of the day was Nikolai's:

"Our whole country is a fortress of peace!"

The words "peace" and "fortress" hardly go together, but sometimes murder will out, inadvertently! The "fortress" part in regard to the Soviet Union contains more truth than poetry. Someone has well said that the Soviets mean to have "peace" even if they have to fight for it!

Love and Brotherhood, Nikolai declared, are brought about through patriotism, defined as absolute faith in what the Soviet Union does.

The most idiotic climax of the entire Nikolai anti-U.S. Hurrah-for-the-USSR ravings came when he orated:

We are inspired to enter this fight by our great and mighty Motherland!

The Soviet Union towers like an impregnable citadel of Peace above the murky waves of a stormy ocean. Our citadel is taller than Mont Blancs and Everests.

In its watchtower constantly stands the first sentinel of peace. Vigilant are his eyes; strong is his hand, which indicates to people the road to life; rhythmically beats his all-embracing heart, which absorbs the pain of all who are in distress; it is filled with restrained but implacable anger against tormentors and with great love for mankind. He will not permit mankind, whom he but recently saved, to be subjected to new torments.

Before we go any further in this adorable eulogy let's try to guess who it is that Nikolai is so moon-struck over. Could it be Sir Galahad re-incarnated? Could it be Alexander the Great? Constantine? Charlemagne? Or, even Santa Claus? No. None of them will fit the bill. There is one, and only one. Let's hear Nikolai reveal the identity. Here are his very words:

"Glory to the Great Stalin!"

The official printed minutes of the conference say:

(Stormy applause rising to an ovation. All rise.)

We could not possibly believe it if it were not there in black and white; but, sure enough, there it is, just as if a sainted knight in shining armor had suddenly descended on a beam of light into their midst. No wonder the Holy Scripture warns:

For such are false apostles, deceitful workers ,transforming themselves into the apostles of Christ. And no marvel; for Satan himself is transformed into an angel of light.   [II Corinthians 11:13, 14]

It must be reiterated at this point that this harangue was delivered by the same man who was courted and welcomed into the fellowship of leaders of the National Council of Churches in the U.S.A., and into the membership of the World Council of Churches. He it was who became an honored guest of the National Council whose leadership brought him to Philadelphia's Independence Hall *after* the speech at Zagorsk!

Chapter VIII
TARGET U. S. A.

Nikolai's attack on the United States was followed in the next three days by the speeches of 36 others whose theme was a tiresome repetition of Nikolai's charges against the United States and his glorification of Stalin and the Soviet Union. Each address sounded as if it had been composed from an outline prepared by the Kremlin Propaganda Bureau and sent to the delegates, before the conference convened, with instructions to follow it.

Without a single exception here is what each address contained:

1. The Soviet Union is the world leader for peace.
2. Stalin is the greatest single leader for peace.
3. The United States is the world leader for war and number one hater of peace.
4. The Americans are destroying helpless people in Korea by bombing and by the use of germ warfare.
5. The Soviet churches must appeal to all the church people of the world to unite under the leadership of the USSR in condemning the United States and

demanding an end to the aggressive acts of the war-mongers.

6. The following demands should be made:

a. Stop bacteriological warfare and ban it.

b. Ban the atom bomb and similar bombs.

c. A peace pact must be signed by the five great powers.

d. Brand as "war criminal" the first nation to use the atomic bomb.

e. Broader trade betwen East and West.

f. Expansion of cultural relations.

g. Support of the World Peace Council. (Soviet organized)

h. Prohibition of war propaganda.

When one reads this list of demands he must keep in mind that Nikolai and his religious cohorts of the USSR had all prefaced these demands with the statement that they never engaged in "politics"! Yet, this list reads almost verbatim like the demands of the Soviet delegation at the UN for years, and the "line" laid down in the official organs of the Communists from Moscow to New York, both foreign and domestic varieties.

The attacks of these religious leaders in Russia on the United States and the glorification of Stalin and the Soviet Union are of such importance that excerpts from each speaker must be given at this point in order to educate the church member in the Free World as to what he must be on the alert for and with whom he is dealing. Then, when Western liberal clerical leaders try to pass these same ones off as being bona fide religious leaders whose word can be trusted, the church people can expose and oppose such attempts.

Here they are in order of performance:

Matsanov (Seventh-Day Adventist) :

The groans of the unfortunate war victims had not grown silent when the imperialists, coveting riches and conquests, began to plot and prepare another, even more horrible war. If one thinks of the atom and hydrogen bombs the American aggressors contemplate using in a future war, it seems as though man has lost all dignity. If we add to this bacteriological means as a weapon of a future war, we must definitely say that culture and mankind itself stand on the brink of doom. The war in Korea must serve as a lesson and warning to us. Let us bear in mind the horrible bombings of peaceful towns and rural communities, hospitals and church edifices! The United States which considers itself a Christian nation acts perfidiously and in an utterly un-Christian manner. Did Christ act like the Americans do in Korea when they drop bombs and disease-causing bacteria on the aged, women and children who are totally guiltless in the war? Awareness of the approaching catastrophe has aroused many millions of men and women who have started to act to avert this calamity. A leading role in this movement belongs to our Soviet Government headed by Joseph Vissarionovich Stalin. We Seventh-Day Adventists in the Soviet Union, fully join in this noble struggle for the preservation of world peace. We address this appeal to our brothers, Seventh-Day Adventists in foreign countries, especially in the United States of America...

Flavian (Russian Old Believer) :

Our people's Government has as its aim not war; it strives not for the enslavement of other nations; all its aspirations center around the welfare of the Soviet People, the creation of a happy, joyous, peaceful life, around peaceful intercourse with all other nations. Notwithstanding the tremendous movement for peace throughout the world, bloodshed is continuing in Korea and the world is threatened to be hurled once again into a cunning strategems of the American moneybags who are plotting another war. It is unfortunate that these people who regard themselves as Christians have forsaken Christ's teaching of love and peace. While calling themselves religious people, they, in reality, no longer worship God, they started to worship ill-gotten wealth—the golden calf, the yellow devil.

On behalf of Old-Believer Christians, we, the Hierarchs of the Old-Believer Church, have raised our voice urging an end to the infamies and bloodshed in Korea. We delegates demand a ban of atomic and bacteriological weapons and the conclusion of a Peace Pact by the five Great Powers.

Melkhisedek (Georgian Orthodox) :

The banner of peace has been raised by the glorious son of the Georgian people, the great Stalin. (Applause)

The Georgian people love him and follow him, the standard-bearer of peace. The great Stalin calls to struggle for peace—and the entire Soviet people follow him. The Georgian Church has prayed for his health and long years of life and will devote all Her efforts to the fight for peace.

The Georgian Church and the Georgian people are outraged at the unparalleled vandalism of the foes of peace —the American imperialists who are using the bacteriological weapon on the territory of Korea and China.

The Georgian Church and the Georgian people are convinced that peace will triumph over war because the great Stalin stands for peace.

Long live the standard-bearer of Peace, the great Stalin!

(Applause.)

Long live the glorious son of our people—the great Stalin! The Georgian Church and the Georgian people proclaim in his honor the Georgian Mraval zhamier, wishing him health and long years of life! (*Stormy applause rising to an ovation.*)

The applause must have been quite *stormy* and the *ovation* a real one with only 74 persons present in the room!

Tikhonov (Pres., Soviet Peace Committee) :

Numbers of men and women of good will fully resolved to defend themselves against the danger of another war, against fresh horrible calamities which are being prepared for mankind by the warmakers from the aggressive American-British bloc.

603,570,000 signatures have been collected to the Appeal of the World Peace Council.

As all peace-loving peoples, the Soviet people are deeply outraged by the monstrous crimes of the American imperialists who are employing bacteriological weapons in Korea and China. Investigations have exposed the criminals, and they shall not escape the Judgment of the wrathful nations. We, as all upright men and women on earth, brand the unprecedented crimes of the American aggressors.

Peace will triumph because it is led by the great champion of Peace, the friend of all progressive humanity, the greatest man of our time—Joseph Vissarionovich Stalin! (*Applause*)

Several questions should be raised at this point: Who collected the 603 plus million signatures? Where did they find a warehouse big enough to store them? How many persons did they employ to count them? Who checked the names to see whether or not they were valid? How long did it take to collect that many? Who conducted the "investigations" in Korea and China?

Tikhonov's entire speech was as phony as they come. No evidence has ever been presented to any competent world body to show that over 603 million signatures have been collected for the Soviet style peace.

The "investigators" in Korea and China which issued the vicious falsehood about the U. S. using germ warfare were Communists. The United States did not then nor has it ever used such elements in any war. That men garbed in religious regalia should perpetrate such a lie from a "peace" platform shows the depths to which Communists will descend in their attempts to enslave the entire world. Well did Our Lord say: "By their fruits ye shall know (judge) them."

Paltarokas (Catholic Bishop of Lithuania, Panevezys Diocese) :

> The capitalist states are building airdromes, military bases, even in foreign lands; they are engaged in militarizing Western Germany and Japan; they are waging war in Korea, Viet-Nam, Indonesia.... They are using bacteriological weapons.... This cannot but be condemned by us out of religious considerations.
> We who belong to different churches and religious denominations express our solidarity with all supporters of peace headed by its standard-bearer—Joseph Vissarionovich Stalin.

Metropolitan Sebastian (Roumanian O r t h o d o x Church) :

> I bring ardent greetings to the entire Soviet people, and to its great leader, Joseph Vissarionovich Stalin, the banner-bearer of the world peace front.
>
> The Roumanian Orthodox Church, and with Her all the other faiths in our land, have voiced and are voicing energetic protest against the iniquities perpetrated, in whatever part of the globe, by the American imperialists, against all their activities which serve to prepare a new world war, and particularly against the employment of the bacteriological weapon in the war with Korea.

Manyenko (Spiritual-Christians of Baku) :

We have gathered together at a time when the brazen

warmongers in the United States of America, Great Britain and other lands are continuing to commit atrocities, are producing enormous quantities of arms, particularly such monstrous types of weapons of mass murder as atom bombs, poison gases and destructive germs. And what are they doing in Korea? For well-nigh two years now they have directed fire, sword and bodily violence not only against the warriors who have risen to the defence of their native land, but also against the very old, against women and babes. These bloodthirsty creatures know not the meaning of compassion. To crown their criminal career the fiendish manhaters have begun to launch lethal germs against the valiant and gallant people of Korea. This has aroused the indignation not of us alone, but of all the people of the earth. The curses of all honest men are flung at these haters of men. These mouthpieces of evil, dishonor and injustice, of every kind dare to raise their hands in prayer to God, dare to count themselves Christians.

The aggressors of the U.S.A. and Great Britain are transforming cities and settlements into fire-swept wastes and deserts and are annihilating the industrious population of Korea. Yonder they are kindling the flames of war; we, on the contrary, are building peace. They are infecting healthy people in Korea and China with deathdealing germs, in an endeavor the more effectively to wipe out the populations of these countries, and they are preparing these mortal horrors for others who run afoul of them. The governments of the U.S.A. and Great Britain are doing all they can to uphold everything in the world that is old, rotten and backward.

It is with tears of fervent feeling that the Spiritual-Christians (Molokans) offer their ardent prayers for Joseph Vissarionovich Stalin, the great leader of nations, the bearer of the banner of peace, and from the bottom of their hearts they wish him long life to the joy of the whole of progressive mankind.

Patriarch George VI (Catholicos of All Armenians) : Mankind today faces the terrible threat of a third world war. But, in opposition to the Anglo-American states which are inciting war, stands the Soviet Union, which is conducting a consistently peaceful policy. The army of the supporters of peace is led by the great and wise leader of humanity, our dear Joseph Vissarionovich Stalin, who with unwavering determination forges the happiness of the peoples.

It is painful to reflect, however, that among the statesmen of the U.S.A. and other capitalist nations there are people motivated by selfish feelings who are ready to destroy all the material and spiritual creations of the human spirit, to lay waste to the world, even to destroy it. These leaders lack an antidote against selfish feelings, lack the sense of humanity and brotherhood which spring from the pursuit of lofty moral virtues.

Khiyaletdinov (Moslem European Council Pres.):

We were horrified to learn from the epistle of Professor Mohammed Making, of Peking University, addressed to the Moslems of the world, of the monstrous crimes perpetrated by the American aggressors, who started employing the bacteriological weapon on the territory of North Korea and Northeast China. Professor Mohammed Making's call on all the Moslems of the world to condemn the American warmongers who have resorted to germ warfare in North Korea and Northeast China has been met with lively response on the part of Moslems in the Soviet Union. The wilful spreading of disease-infected germs with the sole purpose of exterminating peaceful people brings the American imperialists back to the stage of savagery and barbarity.

I protest against their crimes and call upon the Moslems of the world, in the interests of mankind, to force the American cannibals to discontinue the use of bacteriological and chemical weapons and prevent the utilization of atomic energy for the wholesale extermination of people!

We are confident that the peace camp headed by the Soviet Union will triumph over war! Long live the peoples of the world fighting against the imperialist in-

stigators of a new war! Long live our Motherland—
bulwark of Peace throughout the world! Long live the
friend of the working people of the whole world and
champion of Peace and wise Stalin! Amen! (*Applause.*)

On and on, like a phonograph needle stuck in a groove,
went this tirade against the United States and praise of the
"glorious Stalin" and the Soviet Union for three days, by
the orators of the leading religions in Russia and in the
satellites. The same phrases, the same descriptive adjectives
and epithets, were spewed forth by Russian Orthodox, Jewish
Rabbis, Old-Believers, Baptists, Mohammedans, Catholics,
and Buddhists. Even a Dutchman by the name of Hugo van
Dalen got into the act. He apologized to the Communist
religious leaders for the attitude of the West, including his
own country, toward the Soviet and its "peace" efforts. He
praised Stalin for his "gigantic creative work". To read his
speech one would think that the United States is spreading
terror throughout the world until the world is shaking in
its boots at the monster, the United States!

It would be exceedingly boring to recount the same
phraseology by all the speakers at this religious "peace"
conference; but, two speakers should be significantly noted
because of their positions in the religious life of the Soviet
Union, and because of the fact that millions of other adherents of their particular faiths are scattered throughout the
world, and could conceivably be used to do great harm to
the United States and its foreign relations.

The Soviet Union for decades has persecuted the Jewish
people. American Jewish leaders have protested the anti-
semitism of the USSR in pronouncement after pronouncement; therefore, it is astounding to read the words of two
Jewish Rabbis, one from Moscow and the other from Kiev, as
they repeat the base lies and attacks against the United
States, and utter praise for Stalin and the Soviet Union.

Here are the words of Rabbi Solomon Schiffer of the Moscow Choral Synagogue, and of Rabbi Itsko Schechtman of the Kiev Synagogue:

Although in the Soviet Union the Church is separated from the State and we minsters of religion do not engage in politics. .

Jews in the Soviet Union and in all the world must not forget that they owe their salvation to the victory of the valorous Soviet Army headed by the great Stalin.

(Editors note: *What of the "valorous," American, French and British armies, plus Lend-Lease to Russia?*)

Now that the warmongers are preparing a new slaughter, planning to deprive us of the freedoms gained and to destroy them, we Jews, like one man, must enter the ranks of fighters for peace. Together with the other Soviet peoples we Soviet Jews fought in the Great Patriotic War, together with them we are realizing the grand construction projects of Communism. We repudiate the slanderous insinuations against the Soviet Union spread in capitalist countries. They forge atomic bombs and use the germ weapon for the mass extermination of people in the Far East. Bacteriological warfare is a heinous crime against humanity!

May there be Peace throughout the world as wish all men of goodwill headed by the bulwark of Peace, the great Soviet Union, which is led by the standard-bearer of Peace, the leader and inspirer of peace-loving peoples, the great Stalin! Amen! (*Applause.*)

The U.S. imperialists, conducting a cruel and bloody intervention in Korea, have lately resorted to the horrible biological weapon and are spreading death among the thousands of Korea's peaceful and industrious population. In the countries of imperialist reaction the words of peace are banned and fighters for peace are severely persecuted.

Long live the Soviet Union, the bulwark of Peace and of progressive humanity's brightest hopes!

Long live the glorious standard-bearer of Peace, our wise leader Joseph Vissarionovich Stalin! (*Applause.*)

In the light of events which have taken places in Vietnam since this so-called "Peace" conference met in Zagorsk, the speech of the representative of the Central Buddhist Council of the USSR takes on particular significance. Here are the words of Gabzhi Darmayev Lob-san-Nima:

Side by side with the great Soviet people, with all peace-loving people of the earth, march the people of Asia, active fighters for peace.... Buddhists in China, Korea, Viet-Nam (Note!), Mongolia, Tibet, Malaya, India, and other countries.

With the purpose of subjugating the whole of humanity, the instigators of a new world war interfere in the home affairs of other countries, depriving nations of their right to independence and development. Today the whole world knows of the great crime committed by the warmongers in Korea and Northeast China—the crime of using the bacteriological weapon, a horror unprecedented in the history of mankind. By sowing from aircraft the microbes of bubonic plague, cholera, typhus, and other contagious diseases, they threaten to spread epidemics of these death-dealing diseases in the countries of Asia and Europe.

The crime committed by Americans against the people of China and Korea has called forth the indignation and denunciations of people throughout the world.

In August 1950, the Central Buddhist Council, in accordance with the wishes of all devout Buddhists and pious lamas, denounced the bloody crimes of American aggressors in Korea, and in the interest of world peace, sent a demand to the United Nations Security Council that a stop be immediately put to the shedding of blood in Korea, and that all foreign soldiers be withdrawn from Korea.

Woe be to the warmongers. . . . They shall not escape
hell and retribution, and their names shall be loathed
and execrated till the end of time!
Long live the great Stalin, standard-bearer of Peace! (*Applause.*)

The phrase "and that all foreign soldiers be withdrawn"
is a pet one of the Communist propagandists. What they actually mean is that internal Communist subversionists, whom
they have trained, who form puppet armies, and who attack
the anti-communists within the country, and invade their
territory, *vide* Korea and Vietnam, are not "foreign
soldiers". Only the American forces who come to aid the
anti-communist governments, in the form of supplies, military equipment or as advisors, are "foreign soldiers". The
object is to let the Soviet-trained and equipped Communist
puppet armies within the countries subdue the entire countries without opposition.

There is nothing on record to show that these religious
hypocrites, wolves in sheep's clothing, have ever gone on
record deploring one single act or atrocity of the Communists
in any country. They have never passed resolutions deploring
the wholesale murder of untold numbers of Soviet citizens,
including religious leaders, by the bloody Stalin, to whom
they shout "Glory", like so many parrots, in every "peace"
speech. Nowhere, and at no time, have they ever gone on
record as abhorring the wholesale massacre of the Polish officers in the Katyn Forest, indisputable evidence of which was
uncovered by a United States Congressional investigative
team, along with military investigators.

Nothing is said by this group of Red agents about the
hundreds of pastors who were taken out of their pulpits,
imprisoned, tortured and shot by Stalin's NKVD and MGB
henchment, some of whom lived to escape over the borders
and recount their horrifying experiences under oath before

American, British, French and UN commissions.

What makes these Red religious leaders "tick"? First they are puppets of the Kremlin. They jump when the strings are pulled. Their mouths quack like so many ducks when the Kremlin hands them the "line"to proclaim. They are "clouds without water, carried about of winds; trees whose fruit withereth, without fruit, twice dead, plucked up by the roots; raging waves of the sea, foaming out their own shame; wandering stars, to whom is reserved the blackness of darkness for ever; walking after their own lusts; and their mouth speaketh great swelling words, having men's persons in admiration because of advantage." Thus did the writer Jude describe them in his epistle of warning to Christians in the Holy Scriptures.

The most incomprehensible thing of all is: How can Western clergymen take false apostles of this variety to their bosoms, defend them against all critics, and even elect them to ecclesiastical office in Western-originated church councils? Such clergymen can only be discerned as disloyal to Christ, the head of the Church, and to the United States of America where they reside in freedom. Again, the words of Christ must be called to mind: "Beware of false prophets, which come to you in sheep's clothing, but inwardly they are as ravening wolves. Ye shall know (*judge, discern, evaluate*) them by their fruits. Do men gather grapes of thorns, or figs of thistles? Even so every good tree bringeth forth good fruit; but a corrupt tree bringeth forth evil fruit." (St. Matthew 7:15-17)

The rotten fruit of the Communist world conspiracy has been left all over the global landscape. Who can escape the stench of it? Millions of the slaughtered twentieth century Christian martyrs cry out for their blood to be avenged of their communist murderers!

Special attention must be given to the self-styled Baptist leader and delegate to the Zagorsk "Peace" Conference, one Jacov Zhidkov. Because of the important connections this man has had with the Western World, especially the Baptist World Alliance, in which he has held high office, we shall devote an entire chapter to him and his other Soviet puppet Baptists. Here we simply quote from his "peace" speech:

We must state plainly that we believers are at the same time Soviet people and march in step with our dearly beloved Motherland in all her good and praise-worthy undertakings, along the road to culture and progress, towards the common weal. Our country and our people, led by J. V. Stalin, the standard-bearer of peace, unswervingly march at the head of all peace supporters.

But with heartfelt sorrow we must also state that not all the believers in other countries, especially in the U.S.A. and Great Britain, have become conscious that, believing in the same God of Love and Peace, they should, like their brethren believers in the Soviet Union, be advocates, devotees and ardent fighters against the universal catastrophe now facing humanity. Oh, that they, too, saw the vast difference there is between the peaceful construction in the USSR and people's Democracies and the horrifying armament race in the USA, Great Britain and other countries connected with them.

We, Evangelical Christian Baptists of the USSR, call on our coreligionists abroad, especially in the USA and Britain, to join the ranks of the great army of peace champions and, together with all progressive humanity, to work for the establishment of friendship and brotherly love among all the nations of the world, to prevent the kindling of a war conflagration which might turn the world into a heap of ashes. We call on them also to influence their governments to cease the war in Korea, stop the frenzied piling of armaments, especially such as the atomic weapon, poisonous gases and the bacteriological weapon. (*Applause.*)

Note the attempt to influence the United States Government through contacts with Baptists within the United States. This is exactly what Zhidkov has been trying to do through the years, as we shall see in detail later.

After the reading of congratulatory telegrams from such leftist pacifist clergymen in the West as Martin Niemoller and Hewlett Johnson, the conference passed three resolutions unanimously (of course). One was addressed to "The Churches, Religious Associations, The Clergy and Laity and All Religions of the World", the second to the Soviet-originated-and-operated World Peace Council, and the third to the "Glorious" Joseph Vissarionovich Stalin.

The first was in praise of the Soviet Union's leadership for bringing about world peace, and condemnation of the capitalist instigators of war. Here are a few words from the text:

> In condemning American aggression in Korea, we are firmly convinced that all Churches and religious communities of the world are prepared to give vigorous support to the April 1 Appeal of the World Peace Council 'Against Germ Warfare.'
>
> Before war has rebounded on the heads of its wicked makers, let us repudiate the impiety of their war-instigated words and deeds and demand of the governments of the Great Powers the conclusion of a Pact of Peace. Our united efforts in this matter are assisted by the peace policy of the Soviet Union, which at every turn exposes the instigators of another war.

The second was a reiteration of the glorious deeds of the Communists for promoting world peace and the indictment of the big bad boys of the West, peace-haters. The proposals of the World Peace Council were then endorsed in the following language:

While extending the sphere of religious service to the cause of peace, the Churches and religious associations of our country unanimously endorse the proposals of the World Peace Council regarding the conclusion of a Peace Pact among the five Great Powers and regarding the methods of solving such international problems as universal disarmament, the elimination of the seats of war in Korea, Viet-Nam and other parts, the conclusion of peace with Germany and Japan, and also the problem of self-determination of nations and of international ties—cultural and economic.

Of course, these lofty aims are to be accomplished by following the proposals made by the Soviet Union, on her terms. For example, "the seats of war in Korea and Viet-Nam" would be eliminated by pulling out American troops and supplies and letting the Communists take over! This would be a "sure"method for bringing about "peace".

The Third and final resolution in the form of greetings to the grand and glorious originator, promoter and patron of "peace", Joseph Vissarionovich Stalin, was effulgent with praise for this man among men ("manliness"), the accomplishments of the Soviet Union under his "wise" and "beloved" leadership, and his "consistency in pursuing the policy of Peace" in the face of the horrible deeds of the Western nations in stirring up universal trouble, and in their "criminal methods of bacteriological warfare."

When this resolution was read and unanimously adopted, the official minutes of the meeting recorded *"prolonged and stormy applause."* Then, after Metropolitan Nikolai commented on the approval of the resolution through their "warm applause", the scene became almost like that of a demonstration at a national American political convention when the nominee's name has been magically uttered. There was *"prolonged and stormy applause rising to an ovation. The delegates rise."*

No such demonstration was given at the mention of the name of Jesus Christ, what *few* times He was mentioned in this "Peace" conference. The Prince of Peace had obviously been replaced by the new patron saint of Peace, the glorious Joseph Stalin.

In his closing remarks to the conference Alexei set off another demonstration when he said that "the world acknowledges the leader of this noble movement—Joseph Vissarionovich Stalin". (*Stormy prolonged applause rising to an ovation. All rise.*")

A fitting closing to the conference was not a word of prayer or the singing of a sacred hymn, but rather the singing of The Internationale, the National Anthem of the Soviet Union! It began with this and ended with this. Not one word of invocation for Divine help was uttered in the entire conference. It was Joseph Stalin's show from beginning to end, all three days of it. God the Father, the Son Jesus Christ, the Prince of Peace, and the Holy Spirit were left outside. On the basis of Holy Scripture, we don't think that the Holy Trinity would have felt at home in a meeting which began with the Soviet Internationale, glorifying the Atheist State, and eulogies to the Red Tyrant, who persecuted the church, and ended on the same theme.

The religious puppets of the Soviet world have never deviated from the Zagorsk pronouncements and tirades down through the years. The pattern was set, the tune was called, and it continues to play over and over again, through the printed word, through the ether waves, from pupit and seminary platform, through the official minutes of the Russian Orthodox Church, published monthly, and from the lips of the Red wolves in sheep's clothing who visit the United States as the honored guests of American clergymen who either do not care to do their "homework", or who are in sympathy with the aims and purposes of the Soviets.

Chapter IX

JACOV ZHIDKOV AND HIS "BAPTIST" FRIENDS

"But the wicked are like the troubled sea, when it cannot rest, whose waters cast up mire and dirt. There is no peace, saith my God, to the wicked." —Isaiah 57:20, 21

For years Jacov Zhidkov was pastor of the only Baptist Church in Moscow which many a discerning visitor from the Western World has poignantly described as "Exhibit 'A' for gullible Westerners". He has also held the title of Chairman of the All-Union Council of Evangelical Christian Baptists in the USSR. He has been called "Daddy" Zhidkov to distinguish him from his son Michael, who is the actual acting pastor of the Moscow church.

Jacov senior was one of the signers of the infamous cablegram sent to U Thant and a message released through TASS, the official news agency of the Soviet Union, which attacked the American Government for ordering Castro to get the Soviet guided missiles out of Cuba.

Some years ago Zhidkov and two other Soviet "Baptists" paid a visit to Canada. At that time he maintained that he was a free agent and that the Baptists enjoy full religious freedom in the USSR. If what Zhidkov said about himself being "a free agent" is true, then he is doubly responsible for the attacks he has made upon the United States and for his praise of the Soviet Union and Joseph Stalin. His defenders cannot use the excuse that he is under duress and *has* to say and do the things he does.

Ministers who have escaped from the Soviet Union and its satellites told the Canadian press, during the Zhidkov party visit, that they were "communist agents and one is an elite member of the NKVD, otherwise known as the secret police." The elder Zhidkov was accompanied by his son Michael and the Rev. Ilya Ivanov, treasurer of the Baptist Union of the USSR.

In a letter published in 1947 by the American Russian Institute, cited as a Communist front by the then Attorney-General of the United States, Tom Clark, Mr. Zhidkov wrote: "We deeply respect our Soviet government which has given us this complete religious freedom and protects it from any violation whatsoever."

Zhidkov has been editor of the Russian magazine entitled *The Brotherly Messenger,* which was described by the United States Post Office Department as "Found to consist of Communist propaganda" and about which the United States Treasury Department said: "These publications contain all accusations against the United States in connection with the Korean conflict." For a while they were banned from entering the United States on the grounds that they constituted communist propaganda.

In May of 1952 Zhidkov signed a tribute to Joseph Stalin which read as follows:

With the greatest enthusiasm as the representatives of various denominations we turn to you, Joseph Vissarionovich Stalin, to present our greetings and to assure you of our obedience and to wish our best for you. A long, long life for the joy of our people and the joy of the whole peace-loving mankind.

On July 29, 1955, the Baptist World Alliance, meeting in London elected this same Zhidkov as a vice-president. How could an organization, made up overwhelmingly of Baptists outside the Iron Curtain countries, elect such a Red propagandist to such a high office?

During the Christmas Season of 1959 Radio Moscow broadcast an address by Jacov Zhidkov. The broadcast was directed to church members in the United States to pray for disarmament and peace. Obviously, Radio Moscow is not going to put on a speech by Jacov Zhidkov on the subject of peace and disarmament, especially directed to the United States, unless it is for the purpose of serving the aims of the Soviet Union!

Perhaps the greatest propaganda contribution Zhidkov has made on behalf of the Communists was on the occasion of the celebration of the 40th Anniversary of the bloody Bolshevik Revolution of 1917 held in October of 1957. Zhidkov's All Russian Council of Evangelical Christian Baptists sent a greeting to the Soviet Government and called the celebration of the Bolshevik Revolution "the greatest day of contemporary history." The message said further:

The Evangelical Christian Baptists are thankful and praise God that the Soviet government during the course of the past forty years has acted according to the high ideals precious to Christianity.

Was anything so preposterous as this ever uttered before by a so-called Christian or Baptist leader? Did he actually believe that the world had already forgotten the terrible blood baths of the Soviet Union, its purges of the Christian people by the tens of thousands, the destruction of thousands of churches and monasteries, the murder of over a million people in the Ukraine, the sending of human beings in untold numbers to the slave labor camps of Siberia, the crushing of the free nations of Estonia, Latvia, and Lithuania; the subjugation by Red troops of Poland, of East Germany, of Bulgaria, of Hungary, of Roumania, of Czechoslovakia; the financing of the Chinese communists and the North Korean communists in their attacks on South Korea and in the killing of American men? Could we possibly say, by the wildest stretch of the imagination, that this same Soviet government "has acted according to the high ideals precious to Christianity?"

Certainly a person in his right senses could not accept such an evaluation of the actions of the Soviet government for the forty-year period following the revolution, yet this is the statement addressed to the Soviet government by Zhidkov and his crew.

Here is the rest of Zhidkov's statement on this occasion:

While the Christian western world speaks much of its Christian civilization and about the ideals of Christianity, yet in fact, it acts quite contrary to these ideals, a fellowship is daily built up in the USSR, which in all areas of life is recreating the righteousness of the Kingdom of God.

In other words, according to Mr. Zhidkov, black is white and white is black; truth is error and error is truth; sweet is bitter and bitter is sweet. If a Russian propagandist makes the crimes of the Communist State angelic acts, it must be so, because, after all, he is a *religious* man!

As if these outrageous falsehoods about Communist history were not enough, Zhidkov had to add to the statement:

Step by step the Soviet Union is translating into practice the eternal truths. No exploitation of man by man.

Hold everything! What about the thousands of people in the dungeons, and in the concentration camps? Is this "exploitation of man by man", or isn't it? The shooting down of the students who rose up in Budapest, Hungary, who only wanted their freedom from Communist tyranny, free elections, etc., shot down in their own blood by Russian tanks and guns; the rising up of the people of East Berlin against their Russian masters, only to be crushed by more Russian armed might; the escape from East Germany through the barbed wire fences, swimming through canals, jumping out of buildings over the Berlin Wall, to the accompaniment of the rat-a-tat-tat of communist machine gun fire; the fleeing of tens of thousands of Cubans from Fidel Castro's communist "paradise" in Cuba; the defection of former KGB agents and Russian flyers to the West, whose horror stories have been told under oath to U. S. Congressional committees and intelligence agencies; are all of these figments of the imagination, or is Zhidkov possessed of an unclean spirit?

This is the same Zhidkov who attended the Baptist World Alliance meeting in Rio de Janeiro in September of 1960 and addressed the thousands of unsuspecting Baptists from the platform in this manner:

In September of 1959, the Soviet government submitted to the United Nations a declaration for universal and complete peace. This most human declaration can become the only basis which will unite all Christian churches and activities in one direction—to beat all swords into plowshares and all spears into pruning hooks.

Here was delegate Zhidkov from the Zagorsk "Peace" conference of 1952 carrying out before the Baptist World

Alliance the strategems harangued from the platform and put in formal resolutions by this gathering of religious red puppets: "Carry the Soviet peace proposals to the church people outside the Iron Curtain and get them to influence their respective governments to put *our* program into action."

So completely did Zhidkov do the job, that the mesmerized Baptist World Alliance delegates re-elected Zhidkov Vice-President of the Alliance unanimously!

From that triumph on behalf of the Soviet Union he went the following summer of 1961 to Prague, Czechoslovakia to attend the All Christian Peace Assembly as a delegate. The United States Department of State designated the Prague meeting as "purely a communist conference." It was Zhidkov himself who sent out the letters of invitation to the Prague Peace conference to fellow "Baptists" in the Soviet Union and in the satellite states.

Then came the vicious message signed by Zhidkov, Alexei and Vasgen I in October of 1962 attacking the United States when President Kennedy ordered Castro to get the Soviet missiles out of Cuba.

On April 19, 1961 from Moscow, broadcasting in English to North America, was carried a brazen message from a known Secret Police official, one Alexander Karev, who has been masquerading as a Baptist pastor and as the General Secretary of Zhidkov's outfit, the All Russian Council of Evangelical Christian Baptists. Karev has been assistant pastor of Zhidkov's Baptist Church in Moscow. Karev presumed to speak as a "representative of the Christian World." He wanted to know what the attitude of United States Christians was "to the streams of blood that are now being poured out on the island of Cuba and to those guilty of causing the bloodshed."

This man in religious guise, a member of the atheist

communist Secret Police then had the gall to preach so-called "Christianity" to Americans and to say that by conniving at the liberation of Cuba from Castro's communism, "The United States greatly lowers the prestige of Christianity in all countries of the world."

Karev has been identified by Miss Martha Johansson, of the Baptist Missionary Society of Sweden in her book entitled *Where The War Has Been Going On,* as an agent of the Soviet Secret Police. Miss Johansson was a missionary in Estonia during World War II and saw the takeover of that nation by the Russian Communists. Karev had been jailed by the communists and had served a one year sentence when he decided that jail was too much for him. He willingly agreed to become a GPU agent.

In a broadcast on official Moscow radio, Alexander Karev told of his visit to the United States in one of his series of "People to People, Soviet American Meetings on the Cold War." The major conference was held at Dartmouth College in Hanover, New Hampshire, and was organized by Norman Cousins, Editor of *The Saturday Review.* The cost of the conference was paid for by the Ford Foundation. Karev made a propaganda speech for "peace and understanding between our nations" and he called upon "fellow Baptists and other Christians" to promote it. What type of "peace" was Alexander Karev speaking about? The answer is found in the Zagorsk "Peace" conference in which he participated as a delegate—damn the United States and praise the Soviet Union!

Another self-styled Baptist leader of the Soviet Union is one Alexis Stoyan, companion of Zhidkov and Karev. Stoyan accompanied the Russian clerical delegation as sponsored by the National Council of Churches in the USA in their visit of March, 1963 to the United States. Stoyan has been identified as a member of the Secret Police by one of the members of the Voronaeff family and by a fellow member of the Russian delegation, Arthur Mitzkevitch.

Mitzkevitch told Voronaeff that Stoyan does not believe in God, that he curses and swears, that he lives in luxury, and when he is stripped, he displays the powerful muscles of a strong man of the KGB who could take violent action against anyone.

Stoyan was also presented by the Baptist World Alliance, meeting in Rio de Janeiro in 1960, as a youth leader, and as being in charge of Foreign Affairs of the Russian Baptist Church.

The so-called Baptists of Russia have been trying to exploit the racial unrest in the United States, in addition to the "peace" theme, by sending invitations to Negro Baptist leaders to come to the Soviet Union on "preaching missions". One such delegation accepted the invitation and went to the U.S.S.R. for the period of August 11 thru August 22, 1962. This delegation consisted of Dr. Earl L. Harrison of the Shiloh Baptist Church of Washington, D.C.; Rev. Walter Fauntroy, New Bethel Baptist Church, Washington, D.C.; Dr. D. E. King of Louisville, Kentucky; Rev. C. V. Johnson of Chicago; and Rev. S. A. James of San Antonio, Texas. Both King and Fauntroy are members of Martin Luther King's Southern Christian Leadership Conference, and members of the National Baptist Convention of the USA (Negro Baptist group), whose President, Dr. Joseph H. Jackson of Chicago, visited the USSR in 1955.

The reports which have been brought out of the Soviet Union, even by Negro university students from African countries attending school in Moscow, all tell how the communists have tried to exploit the Negro, and that the treatment they received in the USSR was, in many instances, far worse than in some highly publicized sections of the

United States. Continuous complaints were made to Western reporters by these Negro students of the sheer hypocrisy of the communists in the Soviet Union telling the rest of the world that there was no exploitation of man by man in the motherland of communism. They stated that there was discrimination against them exhibited on every hand.

Russia's satellites are not without their "Baptist" leaders, also. The Rev. Stanislav Svec, Czechoslovakian delegate to the Baptist World Alliance meeting in Rio in 1960, was quoted by one of Brazil's leading newspapers, *Jornal do Brasil,* as a member of the Commission for Peace, of the Baptist World Alliance: "As for the clash between the Communist and Capitalist blocs, I believe it will terminate through peaceful co-existence."

How could a communist, who has vowed to destroy what is left of capitalism and to impose communism on the entire world peacefully co-exist with what he has vowed to destroy? How can any "Baptist" believe in peaceful co-existence when the communists have declared over and over again that they are going to destroy the last vestige of capitalism, and that communism will triumph over the entire globe?

The Baptist Union of Czechoslovakia is among churches whose information is handled through a communist publication, known as, *Protestant Churches in Czechoslovakia,* an official propaganda medium of the foreign and information department of the Ecumenical Council of Churches in Czechoslovakia, whose chairman is Dr. Josef Hromadka, No. 1 Communist clergyman of the Soviet satellite states. This is the man who came from Red Czechoslovakia to the World Council of Churches' initial meeting in Amsterdam, August 1948, who has been a member of the Central Committee, governing body, of the World Council.

Hromadka even gained entry to the United States for

the World Council's second international gathering in 1954, promoting the Soviet line from every platform. When he returned to the Iron Curtain satellite of Czechoslovakia he condemned the United States of America in vicious speeches, filled with the most preposterous untruths the human mind could conjure up, and carried this propaganda campaign against the U. S. to East Germany and other Soviet puppet states.

This is the same man who edits the Baptist news in *Protestant Churches in Czechoslovakia,* a publication which reports activities and pronouncements of Czechoslovakian church leaders who advance communist political interests.

The head of Czechoslovakian Baptists ridiculed the reasons given by genuine Czech pastors who refused to submit to the communist regime by declaring:

> They got involved in an activity which had nothing to do with religious and church life, and they misused the confidence which we in our country bestowed upon them.

The Rev. Vaclav Tomes of Prague, also called upon the "German Brethren" for peaceful co-existence with communism. This churchman was spouting the very same line which the Soviet officials in Moscow and in East Berlin have been using in an attempt to get the West Germans to capitulate. If existence with communism is so "peaceful" then why did the Reds erect the Berlin Wall and prevent "peaceful" people from visiting one another?

Mr. Tomes of the Czech Baptist group has commended members of the Baptist Church in Czechoslovakia for support of the communist government in that country. He is chairman of what is called the Baptist Unity of Czechoslovakia. It was Zhidkov of Russia who sent the call out in mid-June of 1961 for the communist-operated International Peace Conference in Prague.

The President of the Baptist Union of Poland for several years was Alexander Kircun who visited the United States in 1957 on a so-called "tour of understanding". He also attended the Baptist World Alliance meeting in Rio de Janeiro in June of 1960 as a delegate from Poland.

Kircun stated on September 20, 1961 that Poland was politically communist but that the church groups are free to carry on their work. He added, "Polish Baptists do not feel that being true to their Christian convictions involves them in conflict with their nation's laws. Therefore, they can be members of the Polish Workers' Party (Communist) while remaining active members of a Baptist Church."

What a convenient arrangement for church people! You can call yourself a "Baptist" in Poland and attend church and belong to the Communist Party of Poland at the same time, and this doesn't involve any conflict at all!

One doesn't have to travel to Poland, however, to find this double standard advocated. At least one religious leader in the United States has approved of the same arrangement. In *Presbyterian Survey,* official monthly magazine of the Southern Presbyterian Church of the U. S., for September 1959, there appeared a section edited by Dr. Ben I. Rose of the Union Theological Seminary of Richmond, Virginia, entitled, "Q & A", meaning Questions and Answers. The readers submitted their questions to Dr. Rose and he answered them, as a professor of religion for his denomination.

Dr. Rose was asked on page 46 of this journal:

What is the view of the Presbyterian Church US concerning members and officers being affiliated with fraternal organizations such as the Masons? Does not the ritual of many of these represent a form of religion which offers hope of salvation without Christ?

Here is Dr. Rose's reply:

Our Church leaves a man free to follow his own conscience in regard to the organizations with which he will
affiliate. He can be a member of a white Citizen's Council or of the NAACP, he can join the Communist Party
or the Republican party and not jeopardize his official
standing as a member or an officer in the Presbyterian
Church US.

To bracket the Communist Party with the Republican
Party, shows that Dr. Rose has never educated himself—
although a professor of religion teaching others—on the
various decisions of all three branches of the United States
Government in regard to the Communist Party. The Mc-
Carran-Walter Internal Security Act of 1950, which states
that the Communist Party is not a political party but is a
foreign conspiracy directed from Moscow in an attempt to
destroy the United States Government and its free institutions, was originated and passed by the Congress in 1950,
supported by the Executive Branch through the testimony
before the Congress by representatives of the Justice Department, and upheld by the United States Supreme Court on
June 5, 1961. That makes it unanimous.

But, Dr. Rose is one of many misguided religious
opinion-moulders of the West who still desire to think of
the Communist Conspiracy in terms of a legitimate political
party.

Here are the words of J. Edgar Hoover, Director of the
Federal Bureau of Investigation on this matter, as given in
his testimony to the U. S. House of Representatives Sub-
Committee on Appropriations, January 24, 1962:

Under the guise of a political organization, the Communist Party, U.S.A. acts as the subsurvient mouthpiece
of international communism with the Kremlin setting
the line to be followed. International issues expedient

to the Soviet Union's stated intent of world domination by communism are rotely echoed throughout our country by the Communist Party, U.S.A.

The U.S. Supreme Court, on June 5, 1961, lifted the thin veil of legitimacy when it judicially affirmed the oft-repeated contention that the Communist Party, U.S.A., is not a legitimate political party but a subversive group directed and controlled by the Soviet Union.

One can expect a religious "Baptist" puppet of the Communists in Poland to expound the line that a person can be a good Christian and a Communist at the same time; but it is rather appalling to find the same thesis being taught by a professor of religion in a responsible editorial and teaching position in a prominent *American* religious denomination! It has been well said that often times those teaching others need to be taught themselves!

Ilya Ivanov has been identified as treasurer of the one and only Baptist Church in Moscow, Zhidkov's headquarters. Ivanov claimed in the eulogy of the Soviet Government on the 40th Anniversary of the 1917 Bolshevik Revolution that the Soviet Government "during the course of the past forty years has acted according to the high ideals precious to Christianity for these are also the ideals inherent in the Gospel and taught by Jesus Christ. A fellowship is daily built up in the U.S.S.R. which in all areas of life is recreating the righteousness of the Kingdom of God."

This is absolute blasphemy saying that the Soviet Government since the bloody Communist Revolution of 1917 has acted according to the high ideals precious to Christianity and that these ideals are "inherent in the Gospel and taught by Jesus Christ." This is mis-using the name and the teachings of the Divine Son of God. The Gospel accounts of our Lord's teachings do not record any such acts or atrocities as committed by the Soviet Union over a period of 40 years in promoting communism. Here, again, is another classic example of how the Communists use religion; in this case, one posing as a "Baptist" official who mingles with Western Baptists at such meetings as the Baptist World Alliance where he can carry on "missionary" activity on behalf of the Communist government he represents!

Still another "Baptist" leader of the Soviet Union is one Ilya Orlov, identified to the West as a Baptist minister in Moscow. In an interview with reporter Eugene Wyatt of the *Nashville Tennessean* he claimed that Baptists were multiplying rapidly in the Soviet Union.

All other reports are to the contrary. United States Government reports which come by way of the embassies, from observers, from newspapermen who have been in the Soviet Union, from exiles, from ministers and church workers who have escaped from behind the Iron Curtain and from church information bureaus in Munich, London, Paris and New York, all show that more and more churches are being closed day after day and that more oppression is being brought upon what religious people there are left. This same Orlov signed the infamous tribute to the Soviet Government upon the occasion of the 40th Anniversary celebration of the Bolshevik Revolution.

Hungary has its "Baptist" leaders also. President of the Baptist Union of Hungary is Lazlo Szabo. Mr. Szabo opened the fourth session of the Baptist World Alliance meeting in Rio in 1960 with prayer. He was introduced as a "good Baptist" from Hungary. Szabo evidently was in good standing with the Communist regime in Hungary, for not only was he head of the "Baptist" group before the Hungarian Revolt of October 1956, but he continued to direct the life of the Baptist Church when the Communists regained their power.

When the people of Hungary rose up against their Communist masters and threw off the yoke of oppression for a few brief days, one of the first things they did was to remove from the pulpits and the seminaries those religious Red puppets who had been installed in their offices by the Communist state regime because of their fealty to the Reds. These puppets were replaced with the true pastors and teachers, that is, those who could be found in the dungeons and underground places of entombment. Some were never found although their cries could be heard above ground as the people diligently searched and dug for them.

The Communists, defeated temporarily, soon counterattacked with the full aid of Soviet armed forces, including tanks and mortars. They mowed down the Freedom Fighters with machinegun fire, murdered thousands of them in the main square of Budapest, and hung hundreds of others in public places, as they regained power without any help from the Western nations coming to the rescue of the patriots.

Having regained their power, the Communists then took the faithful pastors and religious leaders out of their pulpits and schools, incarcerated them once again, and reinstalled the puppets.

The *Hungarian Church Press,* published by the Communists in Budapest, is under the direction of Bishop Lajos Veto, member of the Communist Parliament, a so-called Lutheran, and elected member of the Central Committee of the World Council of Churches.

Szabo, President of the Baptist Union of Hungary, also signed the Declaration of the World Peace Council (Soviet organization), which set forth the Red "peace" line. Opposition to the re-arming of West Germany, opposition to atomic weapons (while the West *only* had them), attacks on the nations of the Free World as being warmongers and haters of "peace", and hailing the Soviet Union as genuine leader for world "peace".

What has been contended by the author of this book, thus far, in regard to the religious situation within the Soviet Union is supported by the personal observations of the pastor of one of the largest Baptist churches in the United States and in the world, Dr. W. A. Criswell of the First Baptist Church of Dallas, Texas.

In the official state paper of the Louisiana Baptist Convention, *Baptist Message,* for September 30, 1965, Dr. Criswell's findings on religion in Russia are recorded as follows:

W. A. Criswell said here on return from abroad that only the intervention of God could save religion in Russia.

The pastor of First Church in Dallas recently returned from a tour of the Soviet Union. He prefaced his remarks in a news conference at the church with the observation that religion in Russia is almost dead.

When asked how God might intervene, Criswell cited the conversion of Constantine, the Roman emperor, whose sympathy with Christianity changed the course of history. Criswell said the same type intervention could take place any day, any hour.

Criswell said his reason for going to the Soviet Union was to "encourage the Christians there in their faith and to see the situation that existed."

"One of the most tragic things," he said, "is the lack of churches in the cities. In a city like Leningrad, a city about the size of Chicago, or Moscow, about the size of New York City, there is only one Baptist church, one Orthodox church and one Seventh Day Adventist church.

"These are the only ones the government allows to be open and they are open only that the government might say there is religious liberty in the Soviet Union.

"The rest have been closed by Soviet decree," he continued, "and there is no cause for optimism. The situation is worsening."

Criswell said there was an underground Baptist movement similar to the catacomb churches of the early Christians, but that it was small.

He said there are slightly more than 500,000 Baptists in Russia and the government knows them all.

"There is no such thing as evangelism," he stated. "The government assigns the pastor to a church and the pastor is paid by the government. The pastors you see are those willing to obey."

"Very few young people are church members," he said, "and there is very little curiosity by the young people in regard to religion. The people who are church members are always suspected by the government and usually suffer a servant type of life."

Criswell said that since there are no seminaries or schools of religion in Russia, each pastor has six to 12 assistants which he trains for the ministry.

He said the Russian Christians had six services a week and each service was characterized by six to 12 special musical numbers. He called the singing great, but said it has a plaintive quality.

"The pastors," he said, "preach in generalities."

Criswell said the one thing the Communists agree on is a bitter hatred of the American way of life.

Dr. Criswell's observations and conclusions are in definite contrast to the propaganda reports issued by the liberal-left leadership of the National and World Councils of Churches, who would have church members in the Free World believe that all is peace and light in the Soviet Union and that the churches are flourishing under communism. Needless to say, Dr. Criswell's observations were not disseminated by this powerful liberal-left religious coalition which always seems to get adequate space in the bulk of religious magazines and secular press within the United States when they make their pro-Soviet propaganda speeches.

Dr. Criswell confirms the absence of more than one Baptist church in the great cities of Russia teeming with millions of persons. Perhaps the leadership of the Baptist World Alliance can explain how it is that they can receive the pastors of these few churches who are assigned to them by the Soviet government, who obey the orders from the Kremlin, but who are elected to positions in the Baptist World Alliance under the guise of being bona fide Baptists and Christians.

Chapter X

NO COMPROMISE
WITH EVIL

"Thou shalt not follow a multitude to do evil."—Exodus
23:2

Dr. Edwin Tuller, General Secretary of the
American Baptist Convention, a full member of the National
and World Councils of Churches, and of the Baptist World
Alliance, tried to explain away the use of religious leaders
in Russia by the Communist government in power by saying
that Soviet church delegations "have to spout peace talk
and discharge an obligation to the USSR government in
order to continue work in Russia, but they know that we
understand this."

Such an attitude is inexcusable in the light of Christian
teaching in the Holy Scriptures. There would have been no
martyrs for the Christian Faith under the Caesars, or other
earthly tyrants in history, if such a position of collaboration
with the anti-Christ or God-less state had been taken by men

and women of faith. They were willing to be burned at the stake, torn by the wild beasts in the Roman arenas, crucified, become flaming torches on poles, or go into the catacombs to worship, rather than capitulate to the demands of the ungodly. These were the stalwarts who gave Christianity its dynamic and which caused it to spread throughout the world. Someone has well said that we have lost that dynamic in the 20th Century because of compromise with evil, and because of this the Christian Faith in many areas is represented by a milk-sopped, spineless group who go along with anything which is expedient. No wonder the Red tide advances steadily over such weak opposition!

We are in an ideological war, not a military one. The struggle for the minds of men is being fought through propaganda, much of it lies and deceit. If ever there was a time in the history of the world when free nations, or what remains of them, needed a dynamic faith to overcome the forces of Satan, that time is now. Such a faith cannot be had through compromise or hypocrisy. That type has no appeal to unconverted millions!

Nowhere in the Bible is compromise with evil taught. Rather, such a position is denounced by the prophets of the Old Testament, the Apostles of the New Testament, and by the Lord Jesus Christ, the Son, and by Jehovah, God the Father, on page after page of Sacred Writ. The words of our Lord as recorded in St. Matthew's Gospel, chapter 23 are classic in this regard. In every verse and in the strongest language He denounced the hypocrites who put on religious regalia, loved to parade before the public as one thing, and behind the façade were something quite different. He referred to these hypocritical religious leaders as "whited sepulchres"—beautiful to look upon on the outside—polished, gleaming, white Italian Carrara marble—but inside, full of dead men's bones and corruption! Christ called them "vipers" (snakes in the grass). He pronounced judgment upon them and warned the people against following them. Yet, these were the religious leaders "recognized" by the State, in dealing through them with the people. They were the ones who were summoned by Pilate, Agrippa, Festus, and the Caesars when they wished to communicate to the people.

Deceitful men have not changed one iota since the First Century A.D. They are basically the same inside. Only the mode of dress, transportation, communication and architecture have changed in some instances. Their methods are as old as time, itself. Neither have the standards of God's righteousness and truth changed. What has happened in our modern world is that men have forsaken God's standards and have substituted their own convenient ones or that which is expedient for the moment. That is why some religious leaders of the Western World can freely hobnob with wolves in sheep's clothing of the Communist world and explain away their hypocrisy and perfidy. What the Western liberal clergymen do not seem to grasp is that this attitude and tolerance on their part is contributing to the Communist plan for the subjugation of the West.

Again we quote Yuri Rastvorov, former agent of the Soviet Secret Police who escaped to the West and told the United States Senate Internal Security Committee as follows, on April 12, 1956:

> As you know, the church in the Soviet Union is not independent as at the present time the Soviet Government is trying to prove. It is completely dependent on the tate and the State conducts all activities of the church in the Soviet Union.

The Pentecostal Evangel, published in the United States, issue of November 27, 1960, contained an interview with

Mrs. Katherine Voronaeff, who was born in Russia, and who, with her husband, was a Christian worker imprisoned by Stalin. She was permitted to come to the United States by Khrushchev after a personal appeal from her son Paul, American minister. Here is part of the interview:

Question: Is it true that the communists are more liberal and tolerant of religion than before?

Answer (by Mrs. Voronaeff): No. The communists have their own religion and still consider Christianity their greatest enemy.

Question: Is it true that any regular pastor preaching in a Russian pulpit must first be a card-carrying communist?

Answer: That is true.

Question: Are Christians being arrested in Russia today?

Answer: I was threatened as late as last June when I made an attempt to speak to a tourist. Recently our full Gospel leaders drew up a petition asking for the right to hold their own services. All of those whose signatures appeared on this petition were arrested and sent to Siberia for twenty-five years.

The Reverend L. Zabko Potapovich, Ukraninian Baptist pastor, now living in Chester, Pennsylvania, who edits the *Ukrainian Baptist Magazine,* stated in September 1955 that so-called religious freedom in the USSR is only on paper. The Baptist Church in Moscow, he declared, is only a show; the congregation consists only of elderly people. There are no Bibles, no hymn books, no Sunday School, or no Bible Conferences. He further states that there are only about one-sixth of the number of Baptists left of the original membership of the 1920's.

Soviet writer, V. G. Sokolov in the publication, the *Friends Intelligencer* for February 10, 1951, writes:

> For example, the All Union Council of Evangelical Baptist Christians in one of its letters to foreign Baptists in 1947 declares flatly that the Russian Baptists 'fully share the social-economic principles of communism as not being contrary to the teaching of our Lord Jesus Christ.'

Evidently Nikita Khrushchev must have had a religious script writer among his speech writers when he came to the United States on tour, as this was the exact thesis he stated during his visit. Nikita was a prime example of lifting a text out of its context in the Scriptures and making it a pretext to expound the communist line. Again, that was to be expected from him; but when clergymen write and say the same, they are not to be questioned, according to the liberals!

It is time for America to stand still for a few hours, to pause and to reconsider Biblical history. We need to go back to the Old Testament Era when God's true prophets, who were in the distinct minority, stood in the great open spaces of Jerusalem, the capital of Israel, and there thundered forth uncompromisingly before kings and queens, their cabinet members and advisors, the princes and the princesses, and the majority of the people, and warned them that if they did not turn away from the big lie of the false prophets, who were in the majority (the school of the prophets in Jerusalem, the seminaries, the councils of churches) who were causing the entire nation to sin and to go after strange gods, isms, and idolatry, and to return to the commandments, the statutes and judgments of the one and only true God Almighty, that He would take a heathen, godless world empire by the name of Babylonia the Great and bring it into the land of Israel to attack their cities; lay waste and burn them to the ground until not one stone was left upon another; and take away the remnant of the people as captives to serve the Babylonians in a foreign land.

The people, brainwashed by the false majority of religious leaders, ridiculed and vilified the true prophets. The rulers sought for their lives, forcing them to live in caves or in the mountains. Elijah was in this group of faithful ones whose message the people would not accept. It is recorded that he went out to a lonely spot on a mountainside one day, seated himself beneath a juniper tree and cried before the Lord:

> It is enough, Lord. Take thou away my life for I alone am left in Israel of the true prophets.

Jeremiah experienced the same frustration. He was called "The Weeping Prophet" who desired to get away from it all after his message had been rejected by the hypnotized people and the rulers. He wanted the Lord to permit him to quit and to find a wayfarer's place in the desert where he could weep for the sins of the people.

Isaiah described the nation as being sick with "putrifying sores" from the sole of the feet to the crown of the head, and that there was no soundness in it. He warned of invasion by a heathen power, resulting in captivity, and the destruction of the land, which would become a waste place, unless the people repented and turned to God.

History, both sacred and secular, records and testifies to the fact that these prophets who were labeled "extremists" in their day by the government officials, by the liberal majority of the religious leadership, and by the masses of people who followed the false leadership, were right and all the rest were wrong. No living soul can rationalize away what happened to a nation that would not listen.

The question now presents itself: Is history repeating itself? Is God preparing another great world power, which is not the object of His affection, any more than Babylon was, to be the instrument of judgment upon a nation founded by

Christian forefathers who went out with a Bible under one arm and a ready musket under the other to carve out so great and noble an experiment as the American Republic, one nation under God? Will the siren songs of the modern false religious prophets lead that same nation to destruction?

The masses of America's church people still have the power to decide.

RECOMMENDED SOURCE MATERIAL

Church and State Under Communism, The   A Special Study, prepared by the Law Library of Congress for the Sub-Committee To Investigate Administration of the Internal Security Act and Other Internal Security Laws of the Committee on the Judiciary, United States Senate, Part I, The U.S.S.R., November 10, 1964, U. S. Government Printing Office.

Church In Soviet Russia, The   by Dr. Matthew Spinka, Oxford University Press, 1956.

Communist Controls On Religious Activity,   Hearing before the Subcommittee To Investigate Administration of the Internal Security Act and Other Internal Security Laws of the Committee On the Judiciary, United States Senate, 86th Congress, First Session, Testimony of Petr S. Deriaban, May 5, 1959, U.S. Government Printing Office.

Crusader,   monthly publication of the American Baptist Convention, Valley Forge, Pennsylvania, issue of October 1958.

Ecumenical Press Service,   World Council of Churches Ecumenical Center, Geneva, Switzerland.

Investigation of Activities in the New York City Area, Parts 5, 6, 7 and 8, Hearing before the House Committee on Un-American Activities, House of Representatives, 83rd Congress, First Session, July 6, 1953, U. S. Government Printing Office.

Journal of the Moscow Patriarchate, The, published monthly in Moscow.

Life,   Issues of March 23, 1959, and September 14, 1959.

News and Views,   official publication of the Church League
of America, 422 North Prospect Street, Wheaton, Illinois
60187.

Proceedings of Conference in Defence of Peace of All
Churches and Religious Associations of the U.S.S.R., held
in Troitse-Sergiyeva Monastery, Zagorsk, published by the
Moscow Patriarchate, 1952.

Russian Orthodox Church, The Organization, Situation,
Activity, published by the Moscow Patriarchate on the occasion of the 40th Anniversary of the re-establishment of
the Patriarchal See.

Soviet Affairs Analysis Service,   Institute for the Study of the
USSR, Mannhardtstrasse 6, Munich 22, Germany.

State of New York Court of Appeals, No. 132, February 1960,
Saint Nicholas Cathedral of the Russian Orthodox Church
of North America, Appellant, vs. Wassil A. Kreshik, as
Dean of Saint Nicholas Cathedral, & ors., &c., Respondents.

Synod of Bishops of the Russian Orthodox Church Outside of
Russia,   75 East 93rd Street, New York 28, N. Y.

The Lord of Peace,   address by Jacov Zhidkov to the Baptist
World Alliance, Rio de Janeiro, Brazil, June 1960.

USSR International Affairs,   U. S. Department of State,
Washington, D. C.

World Outlook,   missions magazine published by the Methodist Church in the United States, January 1963.

INDEX